Coleen

welcome to my world x x

HarperCollins*Publishers*
77–85 Fulham Palace Road,
Hammersmith, London W6 8JB
www.harpercollins.co.uk

First published by HarperCollins*Publishers* 2007
This edition 2008

10 9 8 7 6 5 4 3 2 1

Edited by Harvey Marcus

The publishers would like to thank *Closer* magazine for the use of
the title of Coleen's weekly column 'Welcome to My World'.

A catalogue record of this book is
available from the British Library

ISBN-10   0-00-723612-X
ISBN-13   978-0-00-723612-9

Printed and bound in Great Britain by
Butler and Tanner, Somerset

All photographs supplied courtesy of Coleen McLoughlin with the exception of the
following: p.ii–iii © Sandrine Dulermo & Michael Labica/Celebrity Pictures LTD; p.3
© Tina Korhonen/Retna; p.7 © Sandrine Dulermo & Michael Labica/Celebrity Pictures
LTD; p.23 © Rex Features; p.25 © Mirrorpix; p.31 © UK Press Ltd; p.37 © Eamonn
Clarke; p.45 © Sandrine Dulermo & Michael Labica/Celebrity Pictures LTD; p.59
© Richard Young/Rex Features; p.73 © A Macpherson/ Splash; p.77 © John Chapple/Rex
Features; p.89 © Sandrine Dulermo & Michael Labica/Celebrity Pictures LTD;
p.101 © Mark Campbell/Rex Features; p.111 © Big Pictures; p.115 © Sandrine Dulermo
& Michael Labica/Celebrity Pictures LTD; p.119 © Express Syndication; p.133 © Paul
Cousans; p.149 © Big Pictures; p.165 © Gareth Cattemole/Getty Images; p.173
© Sandrine Dulermo & Michael Labica/Celebrity Pictures LTD; p.179 © Kim
Knott/Marie Claire/IPC+ Syndication; p.185 © Richard Young/ Rex Features; p.190–1 ©
Mirrorpix; p.201 © Longden-Farrell/Xposure; p.217 © Mirrorpix; p.227 © Express
Syndication; p.231 © Sandrine Dulermo & Michael Labica/Celebrity Pictures LTD; p.237
© Eamonn Clarke; p.247 © Dave M Benett/Getty Images; p.255 © Dave Thompson/
AP/Empics; p.260 © Richard Young/ Rex Features; p.273 © Cruise Pictures/Empics;
p.285 © Eamonn Clarke; p.295 © Courtesy of Disney; p.306–307 © photography & art
direction Ellis Parrinder @ PCP agency; p.313 © Fragrance and Beauty Ltd; p.315 © ITV plc;
p.317 © Steve Farrell.

contents

This book is for the people most important to me in life, the ones who matter the most and the ones who have loved and influenced me throughout my life and still do so today.

Mum and Dad

Two very special people who I love very much. Thank you for giving me the life I love and have loved, for the continuous love and support you have always given me and continue to give me.

Our Joe and Anthony

My mates, our kids, the lads! I love you and thanks for all our laughs.

Rosie

You are a very special little girl who has brought so much love and happiness into our family. We all love you x (A sister I thought I would never have.)

Wayne

My friend, my rock, my lover. I love you so much; you mean the world to me. Thanks for just being you!

This book isn't an autobiography, I'm too young to write one of those. Instead it is the story of the last few years and all the experiences I've faced. It's as much about my life as it is my love of fashion, style and beauty. And, of course, shopping! Hopefully I'll be able to tell you what it's really been like living in the spotlight while trying to stay true to myself and my background, and I'll share some of what I've learned along the way. Since the hardback was published, my life has changed even more, so I've updated the story in chapter 21 with what's happened since then, including my new, exciting wedding plans! It really has been every young girl's dream come true.

Welcome to my world.

chapter one

croxteth, baden-baden, monaco, cannes & st tropez

It's the summer of 2006. England's World Cup is over, and me and Wayne are aboard a yacht called *The Willsea*, spending a week sailing round the French Riviera. We flew in to France by private jet, then took a helicopter to Monaco before sailing to St Tropez, then on to Cannes.

After Germany, we just wanted to go somewhere and totally relax. Wayne likes Barbados, that's his favourite holiday spot, but we'd been going there for the last two years and didn't want to travel too far this time, and I wanted to try somewhere in Europe. At the football there had been loads of talk among the wives, girlfriends and players about chartering yachts, because doing this made it much easier to deal with the press attention – or so we thought – and that made our decision.

The Willsea is a 100-foot yacht, with four bedrooms for guests – two double rooms and two singles – all with en suite bathrooms. Upstairs there's a dining room, a living room, a kitchen and another three bedrooms where the staff sleep – the captain, his right-hand man, the cook and two waiters. There are decks where you can sunbathe, eat or do whatever you want. Eight of us are on this trip: me, Wayne, my Auntie Tracy and Uncle Shaun, and two other couples who are friends of ours.

Wayne hates the sun, so when we go away he usually likes to stay in the shade, or he'll go and watch DVDs. The weather has been amazing but he's been quite good on this trip, and I think it's because we're with a group and it's been really enjoyable going out with the others. It's also been nice to have time to ourselves as well, just the two of us lying out in the sun. Of course, Wayne is putting on loads of sun cream to stop himself burning. Factor 40, I think.

It's funny to talk about something being over because we're still so young and things are just starting for both of us.

It's been a relaxing break, which is a relief because the World Cup ended up being stressful. Wayne was gutted about losing, but I told him he'd just got to let it go, there was no point moping around. However, that's easier said than done. For the first few days after he came back from Germany, Wayne was narky – well, he wasn't narky exactly, but he was upset and he didn't want to do anything. I told him that he should leave it behind, because he will have more World Cups coming up, and that one was over now.

It's funny to talk about something being over because we're still so young and things are just starting for both of us. We were only away for a week, but this holiday more than any other, and the weeks in Germany leading up to it, made me think about how much my life has changed over the last few years. Sometimes it's easy to forget, but being away with friends and family makes you take so much more notice of everything – the good and the bad.

It was floating in the middle of the Mediterranean Sea, not far from the beaches of St Tropez, only a couple of days away from going back home to Liverpool, that I decided to start writing this book. I wanted to put down on paper what the last four years have really been like – never mind what you read in the newspapers and the pages of magazines. Because everyone I meet asks me the same question: What has it been like, going from that sixteen-year-old schoolgirl in the lower sixth at St John Bosco High School in Croxteth to the amazing life I'm fortunate to live now? 'That must be an unbelievable feeling,' they say. 'What does that big change feel like?'

That's what I'm always asked, and I have never really answered before. Not what it's honestly been like. Not how it feels deep down to be this ordinary Liverpool girl who, all of a sudden, found myself in the spotlight. Then living this dream, because sometimes it still feels like a dream: appearing in magazines like *Vogue* and *Marie Claire*; waking up to find myself on the front page of the *Sun* and the *Daily Mirror* because the day before I'd been out shopping (*shopping!*); the paparazzi following my every move; columnists from all the different nationals talking about me like they know me. It's a good and bad dream, with the good thankfully outweighing the rest.

I wanted to put down on paper what the last four years have really been like – never mind what you read in the newspapers and the pages of magazines.

Coleen: welcome to my world

This book starts on holiday, after the World Cup in Germany and Baden-Baden, because for the previous month or so it had felt like the so-called WAGs, including me, had been in the newspapers every day, and the life I'd been living for the past four years, all the brilliant things that had happened, had been squeezed into just a few weeks.

Germany had been crazy. All the press attention surrounding the WAGs was unbelievable. The WAGs? I don't even like that label and here I am using it. That's the power of the media. I don't know which newspaper came up with the name in the beginning but it just seems to me like a sneery way of describing all the England footballers' wives and partners. So, from here on in, this is a WAG-free zone! Anyway, back to Germany … People said afterwards that we must be pleased because of the amount of coverage we got, but none of us ever asked for it. Admittedly, some of the girls enjoyed it, but others didn't. I don't know … it was such a weird one, but I don't think we deserved that much attention. The newspapers went over the top, following our every move, detailing how much we were spending, how much we were drinking, the fashion wars. They said there were divides, that there was a competition to see how many column inches each of us could get. Fair enough, some were more interested in that kind of thing than others, but there were never any problems between the girls. Loads of the wives and girlfriends have got kids, so that hinders everyone from all going out together at once.

The fact is, like in any walk of life, you get on better with some people than you do with others. I get on well with Steven Gerrard's wife, Alex, and I think that's because we both come from Liverpool and we have loads in common – but it's also

Coleen: welcome to my world

because the first time I ever went away with England, before the Euros in Portugal in 2004, she was the first girlfriend I met properly and got on well with. I'm friends with Jamie Carragher's wife, Nicola, as well, who's also from Liverpool.

The newspapers went over the top, following our every move, detailing how much we were spending, how much we were drinking, the fashion wars.

Who else did I get on with? Elen, Frank Lampard's girlfriend, I got on really well with her. They've got a little girl, but she had a nanny so Elen could do a lot more than some of the other mothers. Elen is Spanish but also speaks fluent English however, sometimes she didn't understand everyone's accents and just laughed at us.

Then there was Cheryl. Cheryl Tweedy (well, it's Cheryl Cole now). I'd met her at another match a while back but this was her first trip away with the team. A few months before, I'd actually been to see Girls Aloud perform in Manchester and she'd invited us – me, my friend and my cousin – backstage afterwards. She's so funny and has a great sense of humour.

The first time I met Cheryl we were in a box watching one of the England matches. There was me, Victoria Beckham, Paul Robinson's wife Rebecca, and then Cheryl came in all on her own. Victoria saw her and asked her to come and sit with us. People don't appreciate how hard it is to go to a match for the first time when everyone's in little groups and seems to know one other. It's intimidating.

Before the Euros in Portugal in 2004 we had all gone to La Manga in Spain for the build-up to the tournament. I was seventeen years old, and I hadn't flown out with the rest of the wives and girlfriends because I'd had to stay behind in Liverpool to sit my AS exams. So when I arrived Wayne met me at the hotel, helped me take my stuff up to the room and then we went down to the pool. I'd never met any of the girls before, didn't know who anyone was, and Wayne turned round and said, 'Oh, I'm going off to play golf now.' I didn't know anyone, so I said, 'You can't do that!' So Wayne pointed to a group of people lying round the swimming pool and said, ''Ere y'are, go and sit with them over there.'

There were two girls with their boyfriends: one of the couples was the Chelsea footballer Wayne Bridge and his girlfriend, and the other was Everton's James Beattie and his partner. My Wayne went off to play golf for hours and I went over to sit with these people without having a clue what to say. I didn't even know their names. I ended up asking stuff like what day had they turned up at the hotel, even though I knew exactly when they'd arrived – with everyone else! So it's hard when you're the new girl.

My Wayne went off to play golf for hours and I went over to sit with these people without having a clue what to say.

During the World Cup the newspapers made out Cheryl didn't mix with the rest of us and she and Victoria hung out on their own together all the time, but that wasn't the way it was. She might not have come out in the evening all the time but we met up and went out for lunch and she's a lovely girl. Victoria was criticized in the same way. There were headlines saying how she never mixed with anyone. But she was with us in the hotel, and travelled on the coach to matches with us all and the families. We had a great dinner one night, when my best friend Claire came along, but the press don't really want to report that kind of thing. It makes a better story to say there were divisions in the camp.

After the World Cup was all over, the newspapers used us, the wives and girlfriends, as an excuse as to why the team didn't get any further. But that's all it was, an excuse. If England had won the World Cup they would have said that having the wives and girlfriends over in Germany was a good thing. But, let's be honest, the families haven't been allowed to travel with the England team in the past and I can understand if it's true that the FA will not in future be making official arrangements for the girls. But before we start blaming anyone, let's be clear. We've only won the World Cup once and that was in 1966 when we had home advantage. Why were we in the papers so much? It's not that we asked for the attention. If you think about it this was the first World Cup played out in the digital age and the era of celeb-obsessed media. It was a European tournament, only two hours ahead of England, and the photographers with their state-of-the-art technology had no problems meeting their editors' deadlines. From day one, the newspapers decided we were the other story and were going to turn us into headline news whether we liked it or not. As far as the press were concerned the girls were seen as fair game for criticism and sometimes ridicule, and, in the end, easy to blame for England failing to win the tournament.

On the day of what turned out to be England's final match, against Portugal, we had to get up really early in the morning. Everyone was excited, because the further we went in the tournament the more exciting it got. Especially now we were against Portugal, who'd knocked England out in the 2004 European Championship. Everyone was saying that we'd get our revenge and win this one. There was me and Claire, my dad, my granddad, my elder brother Joe, my youngest brother Anthony and my cousin Shaun. We'd taken a vote among the families and decided to go by coach rather than plane. It was about five or six hours to travel from our hotel in Baden-Baden to the ground in Stuttgart.

I remember things that have happened to me – days out, nights on the town, events I've been to, work contracts, modelling shoots – by the clothes I was wearing. In general I've got a terrible memory, but show me a photograph of myself and I'll immediately be able to tell you where I was and what I was doing. It's weird, but I've always been like that.

On the day of the Portugal match it was roasting. I had on this little grey jacket over a vest from one of the high-street stores, black denim shorts and Marc Jacobs wedges. I remember not wanting to wear jeans, as I'd done at previous games, just because it was too hot. However, I didn't travel in those clothes, I went in a Juicy tracksuit. Quite a few of the girls had jogging bottoms on because it was such a long journey to the ground. I know the newspapers said there was competition between the girls as to who could wear the most designer labels but it really wasn't like that. That's not to say you don't check out what everyone else is wearing. That's only natural. It's the kind of thing you do automatically if a girl's wearing something nice or interesting. Well, I do. Wayne tells me off all the time about it. And my mum too. When I was younger she used to say that one of these days I would get a smack! But I don't do it in a horrible way. I'm just interested in fashion. Wayne says that if we're in a restaurant and someone's wearing something I like, I just look and keep looking for ages. He will be talking to me and I'll ignore him until he starts moaning at me to stop staring!

On the day of the Portugal match it was roasting. I had on this little grey jacket over a vest from one of the high-street stores, black denim shorts and Marc Jacobs wedges.

Me and Wayne have this ritual. He always calls me when he's on the coach on the way to the game. I just say good luck and what have you, and that's it. I know before the World Cup there was all this talk about whether he'd be fit enough to play, but Wayne was desperate to make it to Germany and there was never any doubt in his mind that he would go. He just loves playing football. Even in our hotel in Baden-Baden, Wayne would come over for a few hours and he'd be playing football in the room and the corridors with my brother Anthony. They'd both be kicking a ball about, and I'd be saying, 'Come on lads, don't you ever stop!' Luckily they didn't break anything. They were like big kids. So you can imagine what he felt like, what we all felt like, when he was sent off in the Portugal match.

With me in the stand that day was Claire, my best friend and Wayne's cousin, my dad, my granddad and my younger brother Anthony sitting together, then my other brother, Joe, with my cousin sat further down with Wayne's mum and dad, his brother John and Wayne's Uncle Eugene. To be honest, I never saw what actually happened. I'd seen Wayne go over and confront someone and when he does that I get nervous. I watch other people on the football pitch having a go at each other and, much like everyone else, I think it's good entertainment, but when Wayne's doing it I hate it. I was saying to myself, 'Oh, Wayne, pack it in. Don't.' Then the referee calls him over, and I saw him reaching inside his pocket and I thought, 'Oh, he's getting a yellow card.' But then when a red got pulled out the whole stadium just went silent. The place was packed with England fans. All silent. Then the odd one started shouting, then more, until everyone, the whole ground, seemed to be full of England fans booing and having a go at the referee. And I just sat there not knowing what to do.

I could feel everyone looking at me. My dad enjoys a match but he's not the type to get worked up over football, but I heard him screaming, 'Heeey!' Everyone was jeering Ronaldo. Even then I still didn't know what had gone on, so I couldn't say anything.

Then the odd one started shouting, then more, until everyone, the whole ground, seemed to be full of England fans booing and having a go at the referee.

Wayne had been sent off and there were all these people asking if I was all right, and I was just saying, 'Yeah.' That was all I could say. I was in shock really. All I could think about was that Wayne was going to be devastated. He was going to be gutted.

I'd seen him kick some hoarding or the bench or something, and I just thought, 'Oh no.'

Afterwards there were pictures of me in tears all over the newspapers. I was upset, but I never properly cried. I filled up because you just get this horrible feeling inside you. There were people around me crying, saying it wasn't Wayne's fault, that it shouldn't have been a red card. Cheryl Cole ran down to me and said, 'Just don't worry about it, it weren't his fault.'

Everyone was mad at Ronaldo. Phones were going off all around me with messages coming in. I received a text from a friend of mine saying that Ronaldo had just winked at his manager, but at the time I didn't know what that meant. I didn't have a clue. Then, of course, the match went to penalties and when the team lost you just realized that it was five or six hours back to the hotel on the coach, knowing you're going home and our World Cup was all over. You just think, 'What are the lads feeling now?' Wayne phoned me and said everyone was gutted and upset. Ronaldo? Like Wayne said. On the day, they were playing on different teams. They play together for Man United but for those 90 minutes they were internationals representing their countries in the World Cup Finals so both were going to do whatever they could to win. Afterwards the press tried to make out there was a problem between the two of them, but they were texting each other straight after the game.

After England went out of the tournament, me and Wayne flew back to Liverpool. The paparazzi followed us everywhere. We went straight to my mum's house in Croxteth, and because the press know we're either going to be there or at our own house in Cheshire they were sitting outside waiting. We spent a few days at home, then packed to go on holiday. This time around I'd already had most of my stuff ready and washed at the hotel because I knew it was going to be a quick thing coming home and going away before Wayne had to be back at Manchester United for pre-season training. Honestly, usually I'm terrible at packing, leaving it all to the night before. Normally I'll get my mum to help and she'll be the one saying, 'Do you really need that pair of Lanvin leopard-print shoes?' Otherwise I'd end up taking everything. Not that I didn't try to take everything! There were eight of us flying on the jet and the helicopter, and we were limited to one suitcase each, but me and Wayne had the biggest cases!

It's no secret that I like my clothes, and there have been stories in the past about how many bikinis I own.

If I was going away for two weeks then I'd probably take more than fourteen bikinis, but some of those might be ones I'd bought the year before.

We were only in France for a week, but I brought about twelve bikinis with me. I always buy Missoni bikinis – I love their colours and details. Topshop do great bikinis, George at Asda have a lovely range too and then there's always Juicy. That year I had a big thing for sunglasses. I bought loads of pairs – Marc Jacobs, Dolce & Gabbana, Dior – I never thought I'd like the fashion for bigger frames but the Dior ones look nice on me, and Fendi, the aviators. I bought them in a tan colour just as the summer was starting. Kate Moss had the same ones. Great minds think alike, eh! Then I got another pair in dark brown because I wore them all the time.

With the bikinis, like any girl, I do think about my body and I'm always aware of the paparazzi.

All aboard *The Willsea*. Me and Wayne sailing around the south of France in the summer of 2006.

On holiday I tried not to think about them but, to be honest, I hadn't been one hundred per cent happy with the shape I was in and I didn't think I was looking my best.

While we were in Germany I hadn't been eating healthily or going to the gym. There'd be loads of carbs: potatoes and pasta with sauces. There wasn't that much to do, so we'd go out to lunch and have a glass of wine and then go out for an evening meal really late at night. My eating hadn't been normal for a while, but at the end of the day the important thing was getting away and relaxing with Wayne.

It was a great holiday. The idea was to sail around the south of France and drop in on places like Cannes and St Tropez and other ports along the way. One day we'd be in Monaco dancing at Jimmyz nightclub, the next we'd be in a bar in St Tropez watching France and Italy in the World Cup Final. Then we'd sail out to sea to sunbathe or maybe fool around on the jet-skis. We went to outdoor restaurants where the trees were full of fairy lights, really lovely, then clubs like VIP in St Tropez and beach bars like Nikki Beach where magnums of champagne are going round and everyone's dancing until the early hours. We arrived in Cannes on Bastille Day and ate out under the stars at a private table at the end of a jetty in the harbour, while the most amazing firework display you could ever imagine, thousands of rockets, went off above our heads.

One day we'd be in Monaco dancing at Jimmyz nightclub, the next we'd be in a bar in St Tropez watching France and Italy in the World Cup Final.

The whole holiday was fantastic. We'd be in the VIP area of a club, when it wasn't so long ago that I used to go to nightclubs and think, 'Oooh, look at them in the VIP area.' Being with other people made me think about everything all over again and enjoy things through their eyes. All our friends, they would be going, 'Just think, we're doing this, and next week we're back to work.' It's great for me and Wayne to have family and friends like that around us because they bring us back down to earth. We try not to take things for granted but sometimes we forget how lucky we are.

A night to remember with my Auntie Tracy and Uncle Shaun in Jimmyz nightclub, Monaco.

Croxteth, Baden-Baden, Monaco, Cannes & St Tropez **19**

It's lovely to share such experiences with other people, but unfortunately they also get to see the more unpleasant side of being in the spotlight. The speedboats full of paparazzi, constantly circling. Reading stories about us in the newspapers the next day that are just not true. The attention we receive when out for the night, girls coming up to Wayne with no other intention than to make money out of a story.

I'm twenty-one years old now and I've grown up inside and out. I'll always be the girl from Liverpool, but my life has changed in so many ways.

Whenever a girl asks for a photograph, they always say the first shot hasn't worked out so they can have another. Always. Once we came out of a restaurant in Monaco and two girls came up asking to have their picture taken with Wayne. So Wayne posed while it was taken and then they asked for another one. On the second picture one of the girls started putting her arms all around Wayne, and you know that if that photo was sold to the newspapers they could just make up a story. It's hard for Wayne because the fans are so supportive and play such an important part in his working life, but some people have different agendas other than simply having their picture taken with him. On that occasion I got hold of this girl's hand and went, 'You're getting your picture but you don't need to do that!' She was French and asked if I was his girlfriend. I said it didn't matter. In St Tropez it was unbelievable. Things like that make you see how sly people can be. Some girls can be really evil. I trust Wayne but I don't always trust the people he might find himself around. People are so aware of how much money they can make from a small photo these days.

All that happened in just a few weeks, so you can imagine what the last few years have been like. At times it's been crazy, like a fairytale, an amazing journey. I'm no longer the sixteen-year-old girl who appeared in the newspapers for the very first time after walking to school in that knee-length puffa jacket! I'm twenty-one years old now and I've grown up inside and out. I'll always be the girl from Liverpool, but my life has changed in so many ways. And this is my story so far.

chapter two

question: what's my favourite sport? answer: cricket

From the very first day I appeared in the newspapers, people have been talking about my clothes and my fashion. That picture of me in the lower sixth, walking to St John Bosco High School, is always going to be with me. I look at it now and can't help but laugh. It's not something that makes me cringe, or that I'm ashamed about, because that was me back then. A sixteen-year-old, strolling to school with my puffa jacket on.

I'd been going out with Wayne for a good few months by then, and that day he was heading off to play for England. He'd been round to our house in the morning to pick something up, I can't remember what it was, but the paparazzi must have followed him. Not that I was thinking about newspapers or photographers when I set off for school that morning. It was just a normal day. I'd meet up with my friend Kate and the two of us would take the same route as always, maybe chatting about last night's telly or something similar. Then, that day, a man jumped out from behind some bushes and started taking photographs of me. Photographers really do hide behind bushes! He was snapping away, and I was shocked, but what do you do in that kind of situation? I sped up and kept walking. It just felt really weird.

Further up the street there was a block of flats with a car park in front. Kate and I passed it every day. You wouldn't normally look twice at it, except on that day there was a car there with its bonnet open and a man peering inside, fixing his engine or something. That's the way it seemed, except that the moment we walked past, the same man had a camera in his hand, pointing it at me over the top of the car bonnet, clicking away, taking pictures of me.

'That's unbelievable!' That's all I could say. That's all my mates could say when I got to school. There was just this girly panic among my friends, like, what was happening? The buzz and chatter was still going on throughout assembly, so much so that one of the teachers came over to have a word. When she found out what had happened her first thought was to call my mum as soon as possible.

Mum went ballistic, but not quite how I'd imagined. I was on the phone telling her all that had happened that morning and her first worry was whether she would make the front pages the next day! 'What if they got me?' she asked me. 'I've just been on the drive with nothing but my nightie on, pushing the wheelie bin out for the bin men!'

I said, 'Oh, Mum! What do they want a picture of you for? They don't want a picture of you and the wheelie bin.'

Maybe they did! But it made sense at the time and calmed Mum down a little.

But that was the end of the calm. The following Sunday one of the Sunday newspapers had printed a big picture of me. The telephone didn't stop ringing, with aunties and my nan, everyone, calling up asking whether we'd seen it. Me in my puffa jacket right down to my knees and my school uniform underneath. Whatever I feel about the press now, there's no denying that when you see yourself in the newspaper for the first time like that it's an exciting feeling. You laugh at yourself being in this national newspaper, and it's strange, and funny, but it's exciting too. That day, I must have looked at that same picture at least fifty times. At least. But not once did I think what it would mean or what to expect in the years to come.

That was 2003, and although it seems like ages and ages ago it really wasn't that far back. But things were different. In those days I can't remember there being the same interest in footballers' wives and girlfriends. Yeah, there was Victoria and David, and there was *Footballers' Wives* on telly, but in real life the newspapers weren't interested in taking pictures of footballers' girlfriends for no reason – there had to be a story to go with it. Sure, I was seeing Wayne, and the way things were going with us I expected we'd be pictured together at some stage, but no way did I ever expect the press to be interested in just me.

You laugh at yourself being in this national newspaper, and it's strange, and funny, but it's exciting too.

It's comical to see that picture again, and to think of the stories that followed. Back then, the majority of newspapers wrote negatively about my dress sense, yet today the same people describe me as a style icon, and commentators say that the fashion industry closely watches what I wear.

The *Guardian* has said I am 'the leading style icon for British young women today', while the editor of *Vogue*, Alexandra Shulman, who I did a shoot for, once wrote in a newspaper that I was 'a phenomenon of our time'. My word! I'm not sure whether I would go so far as to describe myself as any of those things, but I do love fashion, and always have ever since I can remember.

It's flattering to know that there are young girls and women out there who look at what I'm wearing and are inspired to go for a similar look.

I can never quite get over it when that happens. In Germany, a few of the girls went out for dinner one night and I was wearing a cream Alice Temperley dress with bell sleeves. I didn't realize what an impact that dress had made until I returned home and the girls at Cricket, my favourite shop in Liverpool, told me it had been 'manic'. As soon as the photograph appeared in the newspapers their phone never stopped ringing, with girls wanting the same dress. They could have sold thousands, apparently. In a different situation I'd be one of those girls ringing in. If I see someone else wearing a top or skirt that I really like, I'll be the first to go out and buy it for myself.

Cricket is this top boutique with great labels. Justine, the owner, who's become a friend, is great at saying what's in and helping to put outfits together. She's played a big part in how my style has developed over the past few years. It's not surprising that people knew where to call for the Alice Temperley dress because everyone associates me with Cricket now. Sometimes you'll get girls

Shhhh! Don't tell everyone...

I don't believe in slavishly copying anyone's look from top to toe. The key to creating your own individual style is to borrow from others, add your own ideas into the mix, have confidence in your own fashion sense and, most importantly, have confidence in yourself.

Here are my six golden rules of fashion:

1. Never be afraid to experiment

An item of clothing will never hurt anyone.

2. The more money you spend doesn't necessarily mean the more style you buy

Team up designer with high street and a touch of vintage.

3. Accessorize! Accessorize! Accessorize!

That doesn't mean go all bling, but you can change the accent of an outfit just by adding a simple scarf or necklace.

4. Be true to yourself

Don't be a fashion victim, wear what suits you no matter what the magazines say this season.

5. Less is more

Don't go trying to over-dress in everyday situations. You can look good without looking like you've just stepped out of the pages of a magazine.

6. Have fun

If you look in the mirror and like what you see then that's the only compliment you need.

from as far away as places like Milton Keynes travelling up to Cricket just to see me shopping and have their picture taken with me. I'm really grateful for the support but I do go shy when things like that happen. I just think, 'That's amazing, they've come all that way just to see me!' One time, I was out shopping in Liverpool when a mother and her young teenage daughter ran up asking if they could pose for a photograph with me. They'd been to Cricket and missed me so they thought they'd try one of my other favourite shops. I suppose they had a few to choose from! Things like that make you feel really self-conscious but it's also lovely to know people think that way about you.

I have my own icons who I admire. Kate Moss is always someone I've really loved for her sense of style. With her it just seems so effortless, as though she could wake up in the morning, throw anything on and it would look great. I wish I could do that. Of the other British girls, I'm a big fan of Cat Deeley. I love the way she puts her clothes together. She's always fashionable but she never looks as though she's trying too hard, managing to go out all glammed up but pulling it off in a casual way. Sienna Miller used to be a favourite of mine when she first arrived on the scene – she has the figure to carry off a lot of stuff that I could never get away with. At the moment I really like girls like Lindsay Lohan and Mischa Barton – they've got a lovely ease about everything they wear and they are always introducing new fashions and labels onto the scene.

I'm always looking at magazines for ideas, whether it's *Vogue*, *Elle* or *Marie Claire* for high-end fashion, or mags like *Closer*, who I write my column for, and who are a great source for high-street designs. I really like to mix. If someone asked me to describe my

Coleen: welcome to my world

style I really couldn't pin it down other than to say I'm a real girl's girl when it comes to fashion. I prefer pretty, girly-girl clothes as opposed to going for the drop-dead-sexy look.

In terms of my style, the one thing I'm certain of is that I always go with my own mind. I might love fashion, but I'm not a follower. I'm totally of the view that the most important rule in fashion is believing in what you like and trusting in your own sense of style. All my family and friends will recognize that stubborn streak in me!

If there's a dress or a top that I like, then I'll wear it no matter what other people think. Fashion is all about experimenting, and sometimes you'll experiment and get it wrong, but that's part of the fun of dressing.

Finding your own style is all about trying things out to see what suits you and not being a slave to the latest trend.

You've got to mix things up a little, combine designer with high-street with vintage. I might buy a pair of designer pants, but if I need a plain top I'll go to a high-street store. If you find it's not working when you get home then take it back! As I say, there's nothing wrong with making mistakes. There have been quite a few times that I've looked at myself in a newspaper and thought, 'Why did I wear that?' But hopefully I get it right more times than I get it wrong.

My big bugbear is when the newspapers write that I have a stylist, as though I haven't got a mind of my own and the only reason I'm still not walking around in a five-year-old three-quarter-length puffa jacket from H&M is because someone's told me it's no longer in fashion this month! I don't employ a stylist and it really annoys me when people say otherwise. I remember watching *This Morning* just after I'd signed my contract to front the George at Asda range. There was a big story about how much I was earning and they had a national gossip writer from the *Sun* on the show. She was saying that my stylist had done a great job of transforming me, telling everyone that the way I presented myself, walked and everything, was totally different from the first time I'd met her. The problem is people watching that programme will hear something like that about me and think it's true. A journalist from a national newspaper is on national television telling everyone she knows me, so why would anyone think otherwise? Except it was all made up. I've not been through some expensive Eliza Doolittle transformation. I can dress myself, thank you very much.

That's one of the real downsides of being in the public eye; the way rumour suddenly becomes fact. A newspaper can print a story about you today, then tomorrow the whole wide world believes it's the gospel truth. I'm not blaming the public, because not so long ago I used to believe near enough everything I read in the newspapers. Like everyone else, I used to think there must be some truth there. I'll write more about all the rumours and rubbish that's been said about me later on in this book, but it is really annoying when people believe everything they read, and sometimes I've found myself having to put them right. I always remember sitting in a hairdresser's in Liverpool and I could hear this woman in the back having her hair washed and talking about me. It was around the time when me and Wayne were going through a rough patch and the newspapers were full of me throwing my engagement ring away in the squirrel park near to where we used to live. I was sitting there and the next thing I heard was this woman say, 'Oh yeah, so-and-so's taken the kids to the squirrel park, you know, where that soft girl Coleen McLoughlin threw away her engagement ring!' I'm sure she knew I was listening, which made it all the more annoying. In the mirror, I could see the girl who was washing the woman's hair and she just looked embarrassed. Eventually the girl told her that I was only a few feet away. For once, I couldn't stop myself from putting her right.

'You shouldn't always believe what you read, you know,' I told her.

'Oh, I didn't know you were there!' she said. 'C'mon, then, let's see it!'

She was talking about the ring. I was fuming, but I also felt really ashamed because I could sense everyone in the hairdresser's staring at me. I didn't know what to do, and maybe I should have ignored her, but all I could think of was to prove her wrong. So I showed her my engagement ring, the one I was meant to have chucked away, still on my finger, where it belonged. She just looked and went, 'Ahh, it's lovely, isn't it?' And I went, 'Yeah.' That was it. She never apologized.

I used to gossip about celebrities like everyone else. My mates and I would chat about what so-and-so's been up to, pore over their lives in newspapers and magazines, but now I'm always telling people not to believe what you read unless you know for sure yourself or it's an interview with the person themselves.

I've had an up-and-down relationship with the newspapers. For the past couple of years, ever since I appeared in *Vogue*, on the whole I'd say they've been writing really positive things about my fashion, but in the beginning there was a lot of criticism about the clothes I wore, saying I looked a show, how I was the Queen of Chavs and all that rubbish. I've never really known what a chav is, I don't think anyone knows. They'd criticize me for my Juicy tracksuits and my moon boots, or because I was wearing loads of Burberry. I don't wear loads of Burberry. Not that I've got anything against them because it's a great British fashion brand, but I'm not a slave to any designer. I wouldn't say the criticism upsets me exactly – hey, even I look back on those moon boots and wonder why I ever wore them – though it can get annoying and a bit tiring. Don't get me wrong, I know the press has a job to do. I also understand that the successful careers Wayne and I are lucky to have depend to an extent on media interest and coverage. But I don't believe that gives the media the right to take over your whole life and continually invade family privacy.

I'm more into girly-girl fashions than the sex-siren look!

Everyone seems to have their opinion on my sense of style. Even Wayne. He prefers me in my normal casual stuff, like jeans and a T-shirt. Mind, he has also said that my bum looks massive in my Juicy tracksuit, but I don't take any notice! Wayne just likes me in normal gear. He's not big on me showing a lot of flesh off. Not that I'm much of a one for split skirts and low-cut tops.

Question: what's my favourite sport? Answer: Cricket **35**

I don't really wear short skirts unless I've got tights on, but now and again I wear a top that's cut a bit lower than usual. Or I might wear a chiffon dress or something similar.

It's at those times when Wayne suddenly becomes Mr Fashion Expert! 'I can see your knickers through that!' he'll say to me, or, 'What are you wearing that for?' If he thinks I'm not taking any notice, he'll tell me to go and ask what my dad thinks. That's his ultimate tactic: 'Ask your dad!' The reason is because Wayne knows that if my dad thinks I'm wearing something unsuitable he'll moan to such a degree that I inevitably cave in and change. Not long ago, I'd been invited to a Childline charity do in Liverpool and I had on a sheer white dress. My dad took one look and said, 'You're not going out in that, are you?' In the end, he made such a big fuss about it that I went upstairs and borrowed one of my mum's underskirts. Trouble was, my dress was a bit shorter than the underskirt so I had to chop a few inches off the bottom. All night, frayed cotton was dangling down from under my dress, and every five minutes I had to keep getting a lighter out and burning them off! Very ladylike.

The same thing happened the other week. My mates and I were going to the local pub and I was wearing a white chiffon dress. Dad went on and on about being able to see my knickers, so much so that I nipped upstairs and put another one of Mum's underskirts on. I should keep a few in stock really!

Dad's one of the few people I will listen to when it comes to fashion. Maybe he's one of the expensive styling team of mine that some journalist was referring to!

Fashion is the one subject that people are always writing to me about via my column in *Closer*. I've loved clothes ever since

I can remember. As a young girl I always loved dressing up. When I was really young, I'd be in the post office asking for *Just Seventeen* to look at the fashion pages, and my mum would tell me to change it because it was too old for me. During the summer holidays I'd stay at my nan's house, and every morning we'd go up to the shop for the morning paper and she'd say, 'Go pick a magazine.' And I'd always come back with *OK!* I must have been about eleven years old, but I really enjoyed seeing what all the celebrities were wearing and what their houses looked like. I can still remember seeing photographs of Donatella Versace's home when I was really young, and thinking how amazing it must be to live somewhere like that.

One of the reasons I was so obsessed with *OK!* was because it was also my Auntie Tracy's favourite magazine. Auntie Tracy is my dad's sister, and when I talk of fashion icons there's no one who's had a bigger influence on my style than her. She was always the young auntie – there's never been that many years between us – and she has always looked stylish. Auntie Tracy used to save me her fancy shopping carrier bags so I could use them for my school gym kit and she was also the person who introduced me to Cricket. I was the typical young niece, in awe of my trendy auntie, eyeing up her handbags and the shoes she wore, wishing they were mine. My nan and granddad own a pub, The King's Vault in Garston, and I remember a family party there when my Auntie Tracy came along carrying this little black bag, with a clasp and a long strap, by Moschino. Even though I was only small I remember thinking, 'I can't wait to grow up so I can have a bag like that.' I'm worse than she is now! These days, we've got the same taste in fashion – we've even turned up at matches to watch Wayne wearing the same

Coleen: welcome to my world

clothes, a jumper by See by Chloé. Auntie Tracy's was black and mine was pale pink. If I like something she's wearing I'll go out and buy it, and she does the same with me!

My mum would tell you that when I was a kid and it came to clothes I was an absolute nightmare. All I ever asked for on birthdays or for Christmas would be clothes or shoes, and I would cry and cry until she bought me what I wanted. I was never into Barbies like other girls, I just wanted a good wardrobe! One year it was a black velvet jumper-dress with gold sequins. I must have been about seven years old.

My mum said she would never put me in black. She didn't think a child should wear black. She'll tell you that I screamed and screamed, wanting this special dress for Christmas, until eventually I got what I wanted.

Afterwards, my mum, who was probably tired of my screaming by then, bought me these tights and little black boots to complete the outfit. Very disco! I think it'd be very in now!

My obsession didn't even stop at clothes. At seven years old I started wearing glasses, and I loved them. The optometrist came to school one day to check everyone's eyes, and when I failed my mum thought I'd done so on purpose! 'Do you want to wear glasses, Coleen?' she asked me, thinking I'd made it up to be trendy. I hadn't. I was short-sighted. I might not have wanted glasses to start with, but once I had them there was no stopping me. The first pair I ever bought had multicoloured frames, and from then on I made them my own thing, a way of individualizing my uniform. I always remember a pair of Moschino glasses I owned which had question marks on the arms. They were great but I've got to confess, some of the glasses I wore were bad! These days I wear lenses.

In my early teens I went through a stage when all I wanted to wear were tracksuits. My mum was never really happy about that, she always preferred it when I dressed like a girl. But that was the trend around Liverpool for girls my age – Lacoste tracksuits and nice white trainers. My friends and I used to go out and hang around the shops; in its own way it was our fashion statement. That was part of me, going through those stages every young girl does when she's finding her own style.

My mum and dad always said that while we were at school they would provide for us, so we could devote our time to

Oh! Please! No! Don't!

There are many reasons to get on your mobile and call the fashion police, but here are some pet hates of mine that should be avoided at all costs:

1. Very short skirts with high heels

Unless your name happens to be Beyoncé and you are singing a little song called *Crazy in Love* you have no excuse. It's not sexy.

2. Visible thongs above trousers' waistbands

The modern-day female equivalent of the builder's bum. Very unattractive.

3. Seeing double

If you are appearing on *Strictly Come Dancing* then fine, but otherwise girlfriends and boyfriends should not be seen out wearing matching outfits. Unless they're around six years old, in which case it's officially cute.

4. Cleavage overload

Message to all those girls who take their fashion tips from men's magazines: keep them hidden and keep them guessin'.

5. Silly hats

Equestrian helmets and Pierrot clown cones may be good for fancy dress, but never mistake eccentricity for individuality.

schoolwork and exams. During the summer holidays, I used to go with my Auntie Pat and Auntie Shelagh to clean the chalets at Pontins – the money was good and I'm sure we used to clean more chalets than anyone else! – but when I was sixteen I found myself a Saturday job in New Look in Liverpool.

It was simply that I needed more money to buy clothes for myself. Not only that, but I'd just started seeing Wayne, and his birthday was coming up in October. Then it would be Christmas,

Not a designer bag in sight! Together with (left to right) my cousin Clair and friends Vicky and Rachel during our tracksuit phase.

so I really wanted to earn some extra money to buy him presents. I worked at New Look on Saturdays, and in the run-up to Christmas I'd work late-night Thursdays. Dad used to come and pick me up afterwards because he never liked the idea of me catching the bus home at that time of night.

Because I was interested in fashion it was a great job, and I used to get fifty per cent off all the clothes. My contract meant I had to buy New Look clothes to work in the shop, which I was more than happy about because they used to have a nice designer range by Luella at the time. I really enjoyed the independence the job brought me, and having my own money coming into my bank account. And Wayne got his birthday presents – an Armani cardigan and a pair of wireless headphones.

A couple of years ago, *GMTV's* fashion expert, Caryn Franklin, wrote a kind article in the *Daily Mirror* about me entitled 'The Making of Coleen', saying how I'd made 'the transition from schoolgirl to sophisticate with ease'. I don't know about ease, but it's been fun. The last few years have seen me grow up, and so has my style and fashion sense. It's been a fashion journey that, for better or worse, has taken place in the public eye. As for that first photograph of me, well, if I'd have known I was going to be in the newspapers then maybe, looking back, I might have restyled a few things. For starters, I think I'd have gone for flat ballet shoes with white socks, not the navy ones I was wearing. And I would've had my hair different – a loose ponytail rather than the tight pony I wore at the time. And I'd be wearing a smarter, tailored jacket. The three quarter length hooded puffa jacket would be history. That would be the first thing to go!

chapter three

always a liverpool girl

Before I go any further, maybe I should tell you a little bit about my background. There are six of us in my family: my mum Colette, dad Tony, oldest brother Joe, who's nineteen, then Anthony, who's eighteen, and our little eight-year-old sister, Rosie. You might have seen Rosie on the TV programme I made with Sir Trevor McDonald highlighting the problems of caring for disabled children, a subject close to my heart. Ever since she was born, Rosie has suffered from a rare genetic disorder caller Rett syndrome, which means she needs twenty-four-hour care. We've always had foster children coming to live with us in the house, and Rosie came to us as a two-year-old. We loved her so much we didn't want to let her leave, and my mum and dad adopted her. We're a really close family. Wayne has always spent a lot of time round my mum and dad's house and he has become close to us too.

I was born in Oxford Street Hospital, in Liverpool's city centre, on 3 April 1986. Coleen means 'girl' in Gaelic, it is to Ireland what Sheila is to Australia. I'm not actually named after anyone, but my dad has Irish roots and his granddad came from County Mayo.

My mum was just eighteen when she married my twenty-one-year-old dad, yet it took them seven years of trying to have a baby, and fertility treatment, before I eventually came along. Then, when I finally appeared on the scene, I nearly died.

My earliest memory is of being in hospital with my mum sitting by the bed crying. I was four years old when I caught chicken pox and I was ill for days and not getting any better. Then one night my mum tried to get me out of bed and I couldn't walk properly, I just kept falling over all the time. They called the doctor and as soon as he saw my condition he sent me down to Alder Hey

Who's that girl? And where did she get those very fashionable over-sized sunglasses?

Children's Hospital in Liverpool. There they immediately diagnosed me as having encephalitis (inflammation of the brain) caused by the chicken pox. I was put on all kinds of drips and stuff, and at one point the doctors told my mum and dad that I might not pull through – that I might have only forty-eight hours to live. I've still got those memories of all the family coming to visit me and me crying my head off. Eventually, I came out the other side, but I had to learn how to walk all over again. Now I'm in the fortunate position of being able to help others by being an ambassador and fundraiser for the hospital that did so much to help me.

One of the reasons my mum and dad started fostering was because they'd tried so hard to have kids and when the time was right they decided they wanted to give something back. It was after we'd all started school, and my mum felt she had the time on her hands that could be of benefit to others. They waited until we were at an age when we – Joe, Anthony and I – could understand what fostering meant and what it would mean to the family. They sat us down and discussed fostering with us, and said they would only do it if everyone was happy. We all thought the idea was a good one.

In the beginning, we looked after newborn babies, who would eventually go on to be with couples who couldn't have kids and wanted to adopt. I can't pretend that wasn't sometimes hard on us. We quickly got attached to these kids and it was difficult to see them go, but, like my mum and dad said, we were giving them a good start. That's how we came to have Rosie. At other times we'd have children with disabilities come to stay for the weekend every now and again, to give their parents a rest. At the moment we have this little boy called Jake who's got Down's syndrome. He comes once a month to stay with us – I say 'us' because I spend so much time at my mum and dad's house that it still feels like home.

When my parents first met, my mum was a nursery nurse, but she gave up work to bring up her family. Dad was a bricklayer, but in the end he had to give up because of prolapsed discs in his back, and so now he devotes his time to Rosie, fostering, the local hospital and the church. My dad is quite religious, and religion and the church – we're Roman Catholics – have always

All the posh designer frocks in the world can't compete with the dress I wore at my first Holy Communion.

played a big part in our lives. My first Holy Communion at the age of seven is still a very special memory for me.

However, as much as dad is religious, it's never been something he's imposed on us. At the age of sixteen we were all given the choice of whether we wanted to go to church any more, we weren't forced to go. Nowadays, I don't go as much as I'd like to, but I do go every now and again.

Up until I was four we lived in Garston, where my dad's family comes from, in a two-up, two-down. Then, afterwards, we moved to Croxteth to the council house where my mum had grown up.

The karaoke queen. I could never sing but that didn't stop me trying...

Coleen: welcome to my world

My mum's mum had died of cancer before I was born and my granddad lived on his own. He moved out to be with his girlfriend, and we moved in, but later he came back to live with us. It's always been the family home. In the end, with conversions for Rosie, we had five bedrooms. The house was always full. My mum's got a big family – two brothers and five sisters – and my dad has two brothers and two sisters, and every Saturday all the family used to come and visit. My memories of that house are that it was always busy and warm, like any family home should be. I say 'was' because last year I was lucky enough to be able to buy my mum and dad a new house. It's not that far away from Croxteth, but it has just a little bit more room and privacy. Having said that, Auntie Shelagh and her partner, Mick, are going to rent our old house in Croxteth. I love the thought that Auntie Shelagh's moving in. She used to come and look after me and my brothers whenever my mum and dad took disabled kids to Lourdes and Disneyland when I was younger. Auntie Shelagh moving in just means the house still remains the family home, which is really lovely.

I'll always be a Croxteth girl and Liverpool will always be home. It's a friendly city. Everyone is down to earth and has a great sense of humour. We used to live just on the border between Croxteth and Norris Green, and when I was younger I would hang out in Norris Green, but as I got older I spent more time in Croxteth. I enjoy it up there, I feel safe, and there's always someone you know around. All the neighbours have seen me grow up from a little girl to where I am now. That's great, because I can just go to the shops and people won't treat me as any different from anyone else. It's just normal. When everything in my life isn't always so normal, it's nice to go back there.

I went to school in Croxteth. My primary school was St Teresa's in Norris Green and then I went to St John Bosco High School in Croxteth after that. I always loved school, but I also loved the lesson breaks and chatting with my mates. I wouldn't say I was a brainy kid, but when I tried hard I did well. I was always in the top sets, worked hard, did my homework, and ended up with ten GCSEs – A* in Performing Arts, As in English Language, RE and Technology/Textiles, and Bs in Maths, English Literature, French, Spanish and Science. I was on the Student Council, and involved in loads of different stuff, and in the sixth form the rest of the year voted me Deputy Head Girl. A year before I'd set up the buddy system. It was a counselling service that allowed girls in the younger years who were having problems to come to an older pupil for advice or help instead of going to a teacher. It worked because some kids are scared of taking their problems to a teacher and they would rather talk with someone of their own age.

When I went to see the careers advisor we chatted about what I was going to do in terms of university. For me, the choice was either Performing Arts or Media.

I used to love drama classes. Throughout my school years, if you'd asked me what I wanted to be when I got older I would have told you that my dream was to become an actress. In my first year at school we did musicals like *Calamity Jane* and *The Wizard of Oz*. I was young so I only got little parts – I was an extra in *Calamity Jane* and a munchkin in *The Wizard of Oz*. Later on I was in *The Sound of Music* as one of the von Trapp kids. I used to love it. I'd also go to drama school at night and I had a couple of walk-on parts in *Hollyoaks*. I just loved performing. From the age of 13, I also used to go to dance classes and was part of a dance troupe called

The Harlequin. I would have loved to have gone to stage school, but you have to be good at singing too, so that counted me out. They reckon you can train a voice to sing but, believe me, they couldn't train mine!

These days, one of my favourite ways of relaxing is going to the theatre and seeing a show. It's then that I start thinking about how much I miss that part of my life. Recently, I've had invites to go and speak to the people at *Coronation Street* and do screen tests for *Hollyoaks*, but when I sat down and thought about it, I felt it was something for the future but not for right now. Maybe later on, when the spotlight on me has died down a bit, I might decide to give it a try. At the moment I think it would be hard for people to watch me on screen and see me as anyone other than Coleen McLoughlin.

The Harlequin dance troupe take London by storm. That's me on the back row, fourth from left.

I did think seriously about studying for a degree in Performing Arts, but even then I appreciated how hard the industry is to get into and the need for a back-up plan.

At the time, I was considering looking into teaching and journalism as alternatives. That was the way my life was going. Then, when I went into the lower sixth, I stopped enjoying school as much. By the end of that year I'd started going out with Wayne and things were changing for me. It's not that I began to hate school, it's just that I didn't enjoy it like I used to, I was losing interest and my life outside was changing. By the upper sixth I'd started doing bits and bobs for magazines, and I just thought, 'What's the point in staying here if I'm not going to achieve the marks I'm capable of?' When I told my mum and dad how I felt they understood and were totally supportive. Their main priority was for me to be happy, and they realized I wasn't.

I wouldn't say I'm particularly gifted academically. I had to work really hard to achieve the grades I did, so my parents understood my feelings, and that there was no point staying on if my heart wasn't in it. Telling the teachers was really hard. They tried their best to persuade me to stay but I'd already made my mind up. I got on particularly well with one teacher, Miss Tremarco, who'd been my first-form teacher and took me for Performing Arts, and she sat me down and asked me whether I understood what I was doing. But deep down she knew I would have been miserable had I stayed on. My view then and now is that I can always go back to college one day and study, which is something I might well do, but at the time my life was changing and it made sense to leave. I have no regrets about that. I wouldn't say Wayne was the reason I left school, but he obviously played a big part in my decision.

Wayne Rooney was part of a group of lads who used to hang around a row of shops near to where I lived. Sometimes I would wander past the local shops with my friend Claire, who's Wayne's cousin, and we used to see Wayne and his mates. I got on well with them all but Wayne was the cheeky one. He got it into his head that he wanted to go out with me, so whenever we saw each other he'd come out with one or two chat-up lines. 'Can I have a date?' he would say, or, 'Am I gonna get a date tonight?' My reaction was always the same. I'd never had a boyfriend before so I used to go all shy. 'Oh, I don't know,' I'd say, then I'd head off home with Claire.

I get on with lads but I've never been very good at flirting.

I knew Wayne was good at football, but so were a lot of the lads from where I come from, and they'd be picked for the Everton or Liverpool youth team. Not many of them got anywhere.

Wayne was in the local papers, but only if you followed football, which I didn't, would you have known back then that he was really good. People think Wayne was loaded when I met him but it wasn't like that.

When we first met we'd do the same things as other kids of our age. Like going round the chippy, hanging out at each other's houses, and seeing our mates. Just normal stuff.

Wayne, however, was never going to give up that easily. He'd walk past my house and say, 'I've been waiting for the phone call!' I never had time for boys when I was doing my GCSEs as I was focused on getting good marks. Once they were finished, I finally said yes to Wayne. Well, actually, it wasn't that clear cut. Beforehand I had chatted to my friend Amy-Louise, who used to live across the road from us, not knowing whether I wanted to go on a date with Wayne or not. He was someone I got on well with but he wasn't someone who immediately made me think, 'Yeah, I'd really love to go out with him.'

A couple of weeks later that all changed. One night, Claire and I were on her bike – she was riding it and I was sitting on the back – on our way home, as usual, cycling past the chippy, when the gear chain broke. There was Wayne and a few other lads, my brothers might even have been with him, standing outside the chippy, so we shouted over asking if anyone could fix our bike. I've since learned that Wayne's not exactly Mr Handyman, but he volunteered that night and somehow managed to mend it. Once he'd finished, he asked me out for a date, probably in return for his services! We started talking and the conversation must have been about my drama classes because in the end Wayne wanted to know if I had the film *Grease* on video, and whether he could borrow it. I said I did, and he could, and so he followed us back to my house to pick it up. I can't quite remember how it happened, but once I'd fetched the video the two of us went for a walk and we ended up in the churchyard. That's when we first kissed: around the back of the local church, the Queen of Martyrs. I'm sure he still hasn't returned that *Grease* video.

I'd never had a proper boyfriend before, so my dad was really protective. He's always been protective but in this case he was especially so. Dad used to help run the local boxing club, Croxteth ABA, with Wayne's uncle Ritchie. Wayne used to go to the club and therefore he knew Wayne a little bit through his uncle Ritchie. That wasn't a problem. But now his little girl had a boyfriend, and that was something he hadn't experienced.

On my first date with Wayne we went to the cinema to see *Austin Powers: International Man of Mystery*. I had told my mum of our plans and she told me to ask my dad if I could go. I was sixteen then, so I was old enough to do as I pleased, I suppose. The main reason for asking was because I didn't know whether I was going to get home later than usual. My dad said, 'Who are you going with?' I replied, 'Wayne.' It was the first time I'd mentioned him. 'All right,' said my dad, 'just as long as you sit at the back and he sits at the front!'

Dad needn't have worried. We went with another couple, Wayne's friend Stephen and his girlfriend Kayley. It wasn't really a big date. We were kids, only sixteen. We weren't old enough to go for a drink or a meal like you do when you are older, it was just meeting each other and going to the pictures.

Although I've said I remember everything by what outfit I had on, I can't remember what I was wearing on the night of my first date with Wayne. I remember what Wayne was wearing – jumper and jeans, and a new pair of brown shoes he'd bought specially – but I can't remember what I had on. What I can remember of that night is realizing how much I really did like Wayne. Whether it was love at first sight, I don't know. We'd known each other and been friends for so long that things just seemed to grow gradually.

Over the next few weeks and months it became more serious, until the day came when I said to myself, 'You know what, I really like him.' Which one of us said 'I love you' first? I don't even know. I can't remember. I think it was probably Wayne.

chapter four

dancing the night away with the stars

There I was, spinning round the dance floor, a head full of champagne – but not too much! – and Robbie Williams up on stage, only a few feet away, belting out 'Rock DJ' – or maybe it was 'Let Me Entertain You', I can't quite remember, but it was mad to see him so near. Everyone was on the dance floor enjoying themselves. It's past midnight and you look around and there's P. Diddy, Elle Macpherson and Jade Jagger. You turn again and there's Sharon and Kelly Osbourne. Then around again and there was David and Victoria and half the England team up on their feet, letting themselves go. Robbie sees us and shouts over to Wayne, 'Eh, Wazza! Do you wanna come up and join us?!' It was amazing.

Of all the fantastic parties and red-carpet events I've been fortunate enough to attend over the last few years, one of the very best was David and Victoria Beckham's pre-2006 World Cup party. It was called the 'Full Length and Fabulous' party, and fabulous was the best way to describe it.

Normally, when I'm invited to events, such as the Elle Style Awards or The National Television Awards, I'm hopeless at organizing and leave everything to the last minute. Mainly because you can wear whatever you want. But for David and Victoria's party you had to wear a full-length dress – something I'm not used to wearing because I'm only small – which meant I started planning weeks ahead.

After scouting round places like Harvey Nichols and Selfridges in Manchester, I spoke to Justine at Cricket, and she had to do quite a search through look-books and designer sites on the Internet before we eventually found a beautiful aquamarine-coloured gown by Alice Temperley. That was the hard part. Picking the rest of the outfit was fun. My clutch bag was by Gina and covered in diamanté. Because of the length of the dress I had to go for a shoe with a tall heel. I tried on Christian Louboutin, Marc Jacobs and Pucci, but in the end I went for a pair by Roberto Cavalli that had the same shimmering effect as my bag. I'd worked with the jeweller Boodles before for other events, and they kindly lent me an amazing diamond necklace, which looked unbelievable. I was told it was worth £125,000, which does make a girl feel quite special, if a little worried about losing it.

On the morning of the day itself, Sunday 21 May, my hairstylist Liza, from the Barbara Daly salon in Liverpool, came over to my mum's house, where we were staying, to do my hair. I wanted my hair up to show off the necklace, so we went through a few styles and in the end came up with this modern-beehive look. I've got to admit that when I first saw the bun in the mirror I went, 'Oh no! That's massive!' I liked the idea, but it just felt like I had this big thing on my head! Thankfully, my mum calmed me down and said it suited me. We were travelling down south by private jet and staying in a nearby hotel before heading to David and Victoria's home in Hertfordshire. Taking one look at my new do, Wayne said I'd better watch out going through customs in the airport in case they thought I was smuggling drugs in my hair!

At the hotel, we got dressed and I put my make-up on. I'm not a big fan of wearing loads of make-up, I prefer a more natural look. Usually, while I'm getting ready, Wayne will be telling me to hurry up. If he's ready then he thinks everyone else should be ready.

There were quite a few players staying at the same hotel and we had Rio Ferdinand ringing up asking if Wayne had a spare pair of black socks because he'd forgotten to bring his; then calling back and saying he didn't need them because he'd bought a pair at the service station. Then Wayne had forgotten something, so he had to pick it up from Steven Gerrard. They're all as bad as each other.

If I'm on a normal night out – maybe clubbing with my friends on a Friday or Saturday – then I'll go round to my mum's or my mates' beforehand, dress there and have a little drink before we go. The last thing I'll pack is my handbag. I have the same routine and follow it religiously. In will go my purse, my phone, my keys, a small bottle of perfume, my make-up and chewies. At the moment the perfume could be Chanel's Chance and Viktor & Rolf, but Chanel is my favourite because they do little compact bottles that fit in your bag.

If I've only got a small bag, like the Gina clutch bag, I try to limit my cargo to as little as possible. I never change my make of bronzer or blusher, so it will be St Tropez bronzer, blusher by Nars and a Chanel blusher brush. I'll swap lipstick and lipgloss around. At the moment my favourite is a lip-pump by Pout. I'll take YSL mascara, although I'm not a big fan of mascara

How to look fab and glamorous in an instant

You don't have to spend hours in front of the mirror, trying on the entire contents of your wardrobe, to look great. Sometimes it's the small things that have the biggest impact and turn drab into dazzling in the blink of an eye. For that quick fashion lift, try:

1. **A pair of diamond or diamanté earrings** for an obvious glimmer of elegance.

2. **High heels worn with jeans,** which will immediately turn casual into smart-casual and elevate you in more ways than one.

3. **The right pair of sunglasses** can lend mystery and midnight glam to any outfit, with a mix of rock-star attitude and screen-siren chic.

4. **A sparkly clutch bag.** Simple but effective.

5. **A skinny glitter belt.** Just a touch of disco will give you the sparkle you need for a night out.

6. **Tuck those jeans into your boots.** Let's be honest, what's good for Kate Moss and Madonna is good for everyone else. It's amazing how something so simple can look so sexy.

7. **Loads of necklaces** worn with a simple T-shirt. Part festival-chic, part Mardi Gras, open your jewellery drawer and throw a few on. It looks like you've tried, but the beauty is that it's so simple.

8. **A designer bag** - my personal favourite. They might be expensive but a designer bag is your access-all-areas pass to fashion. Are they looking at me or my bag? Who cares!

as the next day I usually have big black eyes! I like eye make-up by either Nars or MAC. Other than that, I'll always take my chewing gum, green Wrigley's Extra, my credit cards, and a bit of money just in case I need to get a taxi home.

When the time arrived to leave the hotel a car took us to the Beckhams' house. I've been to quite a few big events but I still feel a bit apprehensive about these kinds of things, wondering if anyone I know will have arrived yet, who'll be sat at our table, the usual things. At the entrance the paparazzi were lined up and there was an ITV camera crew filming people entering. As we walked in they asked me who my dress was by and how Wayne's foot was getting on – in case you've forgotten, he'd broken his fourth metatarsal a couple of months before the World Cup and everyone was worried about whether he was going to be fit in time to play.

I'll never get used to the red carpet. The first time I experienced it was at the Pride of Britain awards when there was a wall of paparazzi shouting at me, 'Coleen! Over here! Coleen! Over here! Over here!' In the end I just stood there twisting my head around from side to side and going, 'Wait! Give me a chance!' That whole walk makes me feel really self-conscious. I don't know if I'll ever get used to it. At the National Television Awards, when I was making my documentary for Channel 5, I started thinking, 'What if I stand there and they don't even want to take my picture?'

We'd been to David and Victoria's house for dinner a few years previously, but this time the party was being hosted in a marquee in the grounds. Once inside, it took your breath away. Everything was gorgeous. They are great hosts. At around 7 p.m., just as we arrived, four jets with St George's crosses on their wings flew overhead. There was a soft moss-green carpet leading up to the reception area, decorated with beautiful cream-coloured flowers and scented candles. In the dining area, over 300 guests sat at round tables, and each table had a silver birch tree at its centre, surrounded by an arrangement of lilies, tulips and roses. And they had my and Wayne's favourite wine on the tables – New Zealand Cloudy Bay sauvignon blanc – so we were made up.

It's rare that you'll ever see me and Wayne attending a public event together. We just don't go for that celebrity-couple thing. The Beckhams' World Cup party is one of the few times it's happened.

I arrive at an event like that and still wonder what it's going to be like. I've never been one for wanting to meet celebrities. Lots of people have favourite actors and pop stars, but I'm not really like that, although at the Elle Style Awards I was really star-struck to see Charlize Theron and Mischa Barton. I suppose the only person I'd like to sit down and have a chat to if I ever had the chance to meet her would be Charlotte Church. Just because she seems quite similar to me, she's the same age, and I think we've experienced a comparable amount of attention and scrutiny from the paparazzi and the press even though she has a totally different career to me.

I remember one of the few occasions where we were meant to go to a big do together, I was told I wasn't allowed and ended up being really upset. We'd just started going out together when

Wayne was named as BBC Young Sports Personality of the Year. He was invited down to London to pick up the award and asked me to be there with him. I was only seventeen and I was really excited. It was just before Christmas, so my mum and dad came shopping with me and I bought this little black dress. Then I saw these shoes in Dune, with an ankle strap and diamanté – they were really nice at the time – but they were £120 and I was still at school and my mum said, 'No, you're not getting them, we've just got you the dress.' I'd resigned myself to settling for another pair of shoes, but just before the awards my mum and dad came back from town and they'd bought the ones I'd originally wanted. I couldn't have been more made up. Then, that same night, Wayne came over and said I couldn't go. His manager, David Moyes – Wayne was at Everton at the time – had said he didn't think it was appropriate that I went with Wayne because we were too young. Maybe he didn't want us staying in the hotel together. I was gutted.

I was excited to be going with Wayne to the Beckhams' party. I expected it to be really good, but I imagined it would be quite a low-key affair with people eating and then a little bit of entertainment. That wasn't the case at all. Everyone was really up for a great night, dancing away and enjoying themselves. It was brilliant. I suppose it's not hard to enjoy yourself when there are 350 of you and you've just eaten a meal cooked by Gordon Ramsay and you're being entertained by James Brown and Robbie Williams! Robbie used to be my favourite in Take That. By the way, I never did get the chance to have a few words with Mr Ramsay about how he was rearing a couple of pigs and had apparently named them after me and Wayne. Maybe it was a good job we didn't get to meet!

Sometimes you go to these kinds of parties and everyone is on their best behaviour, but everyone was so relaxed, including Wayne. The next day the newspapers made a big fuss about Wayne dancing on his injured foot. Well, the truth is that I tried to stop him, but Wayne loves dancing and once he gets going there's no holding him back!

Wayne's quite proud of his fancy footwork on the dance floor. At every party we go to he makes a big thing of dancing, doing his thing, flips, the lot, you name it, until people form a circle and start cheering. He loves it! It's his party piece. Actually, he's not a bad dancer, but he'll start doing this flipping and stuff, then the circle will form and all of a sudden he thinks he's Michael Jackson! At Victoria and David's he promised me he was going to behave himself. Then, later on in the night, he started dancing. I'm stood back and I can see this tell-tale little circle starting to form around him. As soon as I saw it I was over there, in the middle, dancing by his side and telling him, 'C'mon, there's a circle forming, you've got to come over here.' Fortunately, I managed to get him out safely before the flips started.

I expected Victoria's party to be really good, but I imagined it would be quite a low-key affair with people eating and then a little bit of entertainment.

For a lot of events I'll take my best friend, Claire, with me. Over time, I've become a bit wiser to the way things work.

I can go out and enjoy myself, but I have forever got to be on my guard because there are always journalists hanging around trying to catch well-known people out, either doing something they're not supposed to or even if they're talking to someone that might make a story. It sounds paranoid, but I'm always aware that journalists might be ear-wigging my conversations, or they'll try to take advantage of Claire if she's standing on her own and start asking her questions. I've come to understand that it's possible to be at a different party from the one that's reported in the newspapers the next day.

I found that out very early on. I had my eighteenth birthday party at the Devonshire Hotel in Liverpool. It was quite hard arranging it because of the football fixtures and fitting dates around Wayne's schedule. In the end, we sorted out a date and it was fantastic. I'd just left school and everyone was there, family and friends, the place was jam-packed. Everyone was up dancing from the beginning. I was given a three-tier cake, decorated with shopping bags from all my favourite stores made out of icing. However, in the end it was a fight that made the headlines the next day. They said there'd been a scrap between my family and Wayne's. That wasn't the truth at all. At the end of the night the bouncers were clearing the room and asked one of Wayne's family to move to a different area. It wasn't a big fight, it was a small argument which turned into a scuffle. Within minutes the police appeared and the whole thing was blown out of all proportion. It was like someone had been ready to call the police and the press, because no sooner had it started than everyone appeared and the story was in the newspapers the next day. I still can't understand how the press and the police were so quick to arrive on the scene. It makes you wonder.

In case of emergencies

Whether you're at a party or spending a night on the town, a girl never knows when she might have to pull in for a beauty pit-stop and make a few on-the-spot repairs. I'm not often this organized, but when I am this is my must-have first-aid beauty kit:

1. ## Dental floss
   For after dinner when you need to service that great smile of yours.

2. ## Cotton buds
   To tidy up mascara and blend creased eye-shadow.

3. ## A tiny bottle of your favourite perfume
   Or a perfume atomizer. Don't go mixing your scent with any freebies that might be on offer in the Ladies.

4. ## Oil blotters
   I know none of us get sweaty – sorry, perspire. But just in case you do, these will make sure your face doesn't resemble a big, shiny, round, sweaty thing!

5. ## Nail file
   Just in case that pedicure doesn't hold out.

6. ## Lip-gloss or Vaseline
   One for the girls who, like me, don't go for lipstick. Stops lips drying out and keeps them plump.

At the Beckhams' party I think the main reason why people were so relaxed is because the press and TV cameras were so controlled. It just meant everyone didn't have to worry so much about what they were or weren't doing or saying. It's not always that way but David and Victoria's party was great in that respect.

One of the highlights was Graham Norton's charity auction. There were all sorts of things to bid for, like a diamond-and-ruby encrusted Jacob watch that belonged to David, which Ashley Cole bought, and an Asprey necklace designed by Victoria. Ozzy Osbourne said he would cook dinner for ten and that was auctioned off, while other guests offered different on-the-spot lots.

I keep all the dresses I've worn to big events, parties and ceremonies – well, the dresses that I've really loved. I have big clear-outs of the rest of my clothes every now and again, and after friends and cousins have had a look at what they'd like, I take the rest to our local charity shop.

Wayne loves his rap – Jay-Z, P. Diddy, Kanye West. So you should have seen his face when P. Diddy stood up and said he would auction off either a weekend in his house in The Hamptons or the chance to spend a day with him in his New York recording studio. I saw Wayne and Rio look at each other across the table and I just knew they were going to go for it. In the end Wayne was bidding against Sharon Osbourne, and managed to win when he shouted out £150,000. One reason I expected Wayne to go that little bit further was because he's really good

Coleen: welcome to my world

when it comes to charity. The other was that I knew there was no way he was going to lose the chance to hang out with P. Diddy and go and party with him at his house. The invitation was for two, so everyone assumed he'd be taking me with him. Quite a few people dropped by the table asking if I was made up at the thought of holidaying with P. Diddy. I looked across at Wayne and Rio and said, 'I'm not even going, it's them two!' I didn't mind at all. They're both into their rap. But Wayne was always bidding for himself and Rio, not, like the newspapers reported the next day, as a present for me! There was also a story that me and Wayne were going to fly over to New York and P. Diddy was going to close the whole of Bloomingdale's and let me have the run of the place to shop. Now, maybe that would have been a bit more interesting!

Of all the parties I've been to, Victoria and David's 'Full Length and Fabulous' must rank as up there with the best. Me and Wayne were almost the last to leave and didn't get back to our hotel until the early hours. Now, that is the sign of a good party!

I keep all the dresses I've worn to big events, parties and ceremonies – well, the dresses that I've really loved. I have big clear-outs of the rest of my clothes every now and again, and after friends and cousins have had a look at what they'd like, I take the rest to our local charity shop. My mum always goes for my shoes because she's the same size as me. It's good to have clear-outs, but I refuse to part with any of my handbags.

Since we moved house I have my own big walk-in wardrobe, so I'm lucky enough to have the space to store all the special dresses that have made it into the news. I'll never throw them away. They are my collection of memories, and in years to come they'll be the best reminder a girl can have of some great times.

chapter five

a very strange relationship

I've had to learn to live my life knowing that around every corner there could be a man, and they are mostly men, with a camera, waiting to leap out and take a photograph of me. Over time, you get used to it and the paparazzi become a part of your day-to-day life. It's a complicated and quite strange relationship, and I would be the first to admit that, in some ways, you could say the paparazzi made me. All those pictures of me out shopping and with my mates brought me to the public's attention. So it could be said that they allowed me to carve out a lucrative career for myself, enabling me to have contracts with the likes of Asda, *Closer* magazine and LG mobile phones. That's been the up-side of the relationship and, in that respect, I've been lucky. But at the same time I've never been someone who's courted publicity. And while I say you get used to being constantly followed by the paparazzi, that doesn't mean you enjoy it. Sometimes I think it's crazy. Do people really want to see another picture of me carting a load of shopping bags about town?

Each morning I wake up knowing there'll probably be paparazzi waiting in their cars outside the house. They don't tend to follow Wayne as much because they know all he's going to do is leave home, drive off to training at Manchester United and then make the same journey back a few hours later. Whereas they don't know what I'm up to, so they'll follow me just in case I'm doing anything interesting. Most of the time I'm really not doing anything very interesting, believe me, but that doesn't stop them. In fact, some of the photographers are under contracts to capture as many as ten pictures of me per day, so their job is to grab those photos no matter what.

There was one paparazzo who kept on following me all the time. Everywhere I went he was there, trailing me, jumping red lights to keep on my tail and generally acting like a real idiot. One day, when I was with Wayne, he followed us onto the motorway. Wayne is more likely to lose his temper at that kind of thing than I am, so he pulled the car over onto the hard shoulder. The photographer slowed and pulled up behind us. Wayne drove off and the man started following us again.

By now Wayne had had enough, so he pulled up alongside the photographer's car, asked him what he was playing at, and the two of them started arguing. The photographer just didn't care. All he kept repeating was that he was just doing his job! Unbelievable!

And there's nothing you can do to stop them. On another occasion we even drove to a police station and the photographer followed us there. That didn't make any difference. As long as there's a camera in the car the police can't do a thing to help you. As far as the law is concerned the camera means he's a photographer and not a stalker. How crazy is that?

Sometimes the situation is downright ridiculous. I was in one of the card shops in Liverpool city centre, just before Valentine's

Day, and my mate and I were engrossed in looking through the rows of cards. The next minute, we turn round and the whole shop window is full of people peering in at us. There was a crowd of shoppers, three to four deep, craning their necks to see who was inside Clinton's card shop. At the front of the pack there were three paparazzi taking pictures of us, while everyone else had just stopped to see what the fuss was all about. Me and my mate just burst out laughing, and I was thinking, 'Oh, please, I hope I haven't picked up any dirty cards or anything!' People had their camera phones out and everything. It was really embarrassing! I felt ashamed to walk out of the shop. 'You know what,' I said to my mate, 'I'm gonna walk out and people will be expecting someone really big to be in here, like Elton John or something, and then I'll walk out and it's just me!' The next moment, a security guard asked if we wanted to leave via a back route, so we ended up going down some stairs and coming out of Boots next door. Outside I bumped into an old mate I used to go dancing with in Liverpool. She said, 'Coleen! I've just been standing outside that shop wondering, "Who's in there?" Then I looked and it was you!' I told her I felt embarrassed. Stuff like that just makes you think, 'That's so ridiculous!' It's madness. What most people don't realize is that there are now literally thousands of untrained guys out there with cameras calling themselves paparazzi. Many of them have never even sold a picture, but they keep on trying to make money by stalking celebrities 24 hours a day, hoping something will happen that will make their fortune. A lot of them are good guys, but some are really intrusive and even try to wind us up just to get a picture and story showing Wayne or me getting cross. Which anyone would if they were wound up like some of these guys can do.

When we were in Germany the press stalked us everywhere. We'd step outside the hotel to go to buy lunch or just to go for a walk and they'd be with us all the time. In the end, I used to ask them, 'Aren't you bored? Aren't people in England bored of us? It's ridiculous.' Believe it or not, there are even times when I feel sorry for them and I think they're just doing their job. But then in other situations, like when we're on holiday, I wish they would go away, leave us in peace and give us a bit of privacy.

Barbados, 2004. Just me, Wayne and a photographer in the distance. Very romantic.

We've been sitting on beaches in Dubai and Barbados and we can see the paparazzi there, twenty or thirty metres away, just waiting to get a shot of us. It's a public beach so there's nothing we can do. I try not to let it affect me but I'm totally aware of the kinds of shots they're after and, like any girl, it does make me feel self-conscious about my body. I find myself breathing in a bit when I stand up so I end up sitting down on the lounger all day. Otherwise, I take a walk down the length of the beach and there will be a load of them following me. It just means I'm on my guard all day. However hard I try, sometimes I can't avoid giving them the shot they're looking for.

I'd rather just go on holiday and be myself and not care what everyone thinks.

We were on a beach in Barbados once, with a few friends, and I stood up to remove my shorts because I had my bikini on underneath. As I was taking them off I accidentally pulled the string of my bikini and they came down a bit. I just panicked thinking that was the picture that would be in the newspapers the next day.

The alternative to all this is to agree to do a 'set up' with the photographers. If we agree then they promise to leave us alone for the rest of the day. Celebrities do this all the time. The picture will appear in the newspaper and readers think it's a genuine paparazzi shot, but in reality it's all been posed and agreed on. More often than not the photographic agencies will pay money for the picture and often split the proceeds with the celebrity. You can always spot the beach set-ups in the newspapers. They're the ones with the soap stars looking all beautiful and toned, or splashing about in the sea. They're not the ones of them sitting on their sun-loungers eating a burger, or where they have a few rolls of flesh on display. I couldn't pose for one of those photographs. I'd rather just go on holiday and be myself and not care what everyone thinks.

Only once have me and Wayne agreed to do a set-up shot. We were in *OK!* in the beginning, and we gave all the money from that to charity, but that's a different kind of shoot. The only paparazzi set-up we've agreed to was during a few days' break in New York after the Euro 2004 tournament. The tournament had made Wayne into a superstar, even though in the end he'd broken his foot. We simply wanted to escape for a few days. If only. Everyone wanted our picture, and there was a pack of fifteen paparazzi stalking our every move. It was doing our heads in. When one offered to set up a deal, we initially said no. But the attention was getting worse and worse, and Wayne said, 'Let's get it over with.' Our agent spoke to a photographic agency in London, and we reluctantly agreed to do a set-up in Central Park with the two of us taking a ride in a horse and carriage. The whole thing took five minutes, then afterwards they left us alone. It was so simple that you can understand why some celebrities agree to these kinds of deals all the time. After all, you do want to keep some private life to yourself.

Once you start that game, you've no right to have a go if the paparazzi start following you when you don't want them to.

We've been offered a small fortune by newspapers and magazines who would like to come into our house in Cheshire and do photo-shoots. We'll never allow that to happen. My home is the one part of my life that's totally private, which is for me and Wayne, family and friends only. If you let the press inside your home then I think they've got every right to sit outside your gates each morning. I feel the same way about allowing the newspapers to take photographs of your kids. If you allow your child to be featured in a photo-shoot, then I think you forego your right to turn around on another day and tell a photographer to leave your children alone.

We try to control things as best we can, but while I have nothing against the paparazzi personally, there are some who will go to any sleazy lengths to get their picture. In Germany, one night we were walking home from a bar – me, the girls and their families – and the photographers were there with us every step of the way. There was one in particular who followed us everywhere. We'd had a great time dancing and we were just heading back to the hotel. The next day, we woke up to see a picture of me, walking back, minding my own business, while behind me was a man wearing a Rooney England shirt with his shorts at his ankles, flashing his bum. The headline said, 'Rooney Pulling a Moony'. I knew exactly who'd taken it. Not only that, but he'd set the shot up with his mate, another photographer, posing as the England supporter, and split the money. They must have earned loads from that photo because it went everywhere, not just in newspapers back home but around the world. When I saw the photographer the next day he was apologetic, saying he'd give the money he'd made to charity. I didn't believe him and said he could stick it. I never want to deal with people like that.

These days everyone, the press and the public, knows the value of a photograph. So if you're in the public eye you're forever aware that there's a price on your head, so to speak, and there are, unfortunately, people out there who don't think twice about doing the dirty on you in order to make some easy cash.

It's just so easy for a photograph taken in all innocence to be twisted round once it appears in the press. That's why although I'll stop to have my picture taken with a girl, I won't always do the same if it's a lad. If I'm with the girls on a night out and a lad asks for a photograph I'll make sure one of my mates stands in the pictures with us. I've been hurt once in a situation like that, but never again.

On that occasion I'd gone on holiday with my mates to Tenerife and we ended up spending a lot of time in an English bar called Linekers. We had good fun there. Every night there would be dancing and when certain songs came on all the bar staff would join in – it was real holiday stuff. One night we were dancing and everyone was holding hands doing that kind of Mexican Wave, worm-dance thing. Someone took a picture, sold it to the newspapers, and the way it was cropped made it seem as though there was just me and the barman holding hands. The story made out as if I was flirting with this barman behind Wayne's back. What a load of rubbish!

Wayne was away with England at the time and as soon as he saw the photo he phoned me, saying, 'What's all this in the newspapers?' He wasn't happy, and in the end I put the phone down on him. I turned to my mate, saying, 'That's not like him,

he never usually kicks off and starts shouting.' I was worried. We were arguing over something that was totally fabricated. A few minutes later Wayne rang back and told me he was winding me up, but was then worried because I was upset. He knew nothing had gone on, and he could tell that all I was doing out there was having a laugh and dancing, because that's what I'm like. Still, the newspapers came up with their own story. Apparently, Wayne had been on the phone telling me to come home straight away. He didn't.

We did come home early, but that was down to the newspapers, not Wayne. All of a sudden the whole place seemed to be full of British paparazzi, and then there was one incident that tipped me over the edge. The tourists had obviously cottoned on to a way of making easy money. We were walking round the shops when a lad in an England shirt came over and asked to have his picture taken with me. Pointing to all the photographers, I explained to him that I couldn't with all the cameras there. The next minute he runs up to me, grabs hold of my neck and tries to kiss me for the photographers. I didn't know what to do. In the end I was trying to hit him with my bag and my mates jumped on him too. I'm not sure if the photographers had set the whole thing up or not. I was crying and upset and it was then that I thought, 'I've got to go home.'

My friends are always thinking of me and I'm forever grateful.

Thankfully, I've got really good mates who understood what I was going through. They're really protective. They don't like the paparazzi and are always looking out for me. It's bad I know, but sometimes if I'm out shopping I'll park on a yellow line or in a loading bay because it's easier than having the press follow me to and from the car park. One of my friends will nip out of the shop to see if I've got a parking ticket, just to make sure the paps don't snatch a shot of me peeling the ticket off the windscreen. My friends are always thinking of me and I'm forever grateful. It's not as if they've escaped the attention of the press themselves.

With the girls on our last day of school at St John Bosco High School, Croxteth.

In the beginning, when they first started appearing in the newspapers, they thought it was a laugh, but it was different because the focus wasn't on them. Then, after my twentieth birthday party at Lounge Ten in Manchester, the *Daily Mail* ran a really nasty piece about them.

I know from my own experience that a photograph doesn't always tell the whole truth. You can be pictured coming out of a club having only had a couple of glasses of wine, and you might

Oh what a night… with the girl gang at my twentieth birthday party.

Coleen: welcome to my world

just be blinking, but that's the shot they use because it looks like you're blind drunk.

On my twentieth all the girls were snapped going into the restaurant and the article tore into them, about their dress sense, the way they looked, calling them chubby and everything. It was really horrible and nasty. They were upset and I was really annoyed. It's one thing to criticize me, but I accept that I put myself out there. They don't. Ever since then, my mates have changed the way they think of the paparazzi. It was the first time they'd experienced that kind of scrutiny and plain bitchiness. There are times now when they run ahead of me rather than risk the thought of being ridiculed in the next day's press. That's awful. They've never felt the need to do that before and it's not right. Why should their lives be affected just because they're friends with me?

People say you can become addicted to publicity and being in the newspapers. I'm not like that.

chapter six

the *vogue* shoot that almost never happened

In 2005 I appeared in the June issue of *Vogue* magazine. On the cover was Hollywood actress and Oscar winner Cate Blanchett and inside was a six-page story on me, featuring some of the most beautiful photographs I've ever had taken. Before the magazine even went on sale it caused quite a storm in the press. Here was the so-called Queen of Chav, as some of the unkinder newspapers had labelled me, being given room in what everyone regards as the undisputed fashion bible. Some people couldn't quite get their heads around why the magazine had chosen to feature me. There were rumours that the shoot was taking place in Cyprus, and that either Wayne or I had funded the whole production ourselves, that we were paying for the privilege of me being on the pages of *Vogue* magazine. None of which was remotely true.

Such was the furore that the Editor of *Vogue*, Alexandra Shulman, wrote a column explaining her decision to invite me to be in her magazine. It made for flattering reading. She spoke of the magazine's reputation for featuring contemporary culture and that it was their job to record what was going on in the world of glamour, style and fashion. I was, apparently, part of a new breed of girls – I was still only eighteen years old at the time – whose style and shopping habits were increasing the awareness of designer brands and changing the face of shopping. She went on to describe me as a fashion phenomenon.

But the *Vogue* shoot so nearly didn't happen. When the magazine first made their approach to Paul, both my and Wayne's agent, I turned them down. Although I'm a big fan of the magazine, at that time in my life I didn't care who it was. I didn't care if I never talked to the press ever again.

> It just felt like my whole world was changing and everything was up in the air.

After the European Championships in 2004, me and Wayne had flown off on holiday to Barbados. Despite breaking his foot, Wayne had really made his name in Portugal and the press attention was unbelievable – even more so because over the summer he'd decided to leave the team he'd been with since he was nine years old. His manager at Everton wouldn't let him leave unless he put in a transfer request, so there'd been a big deal about that. Then there was talk of him going to either Newcastle United or Manchester United. Nothing was settled, which meant I didn't know where we were going to live. Newcastle just seemed too far away from home and family and I didn't want to go there. If that was the case then imagine how I felt about the news that a move to Real Madrid was a real possibility. It just felt like my whole world was changing and everything was up in the air.

Then when we returned home to Croxteth from holiday in Barbados, Wayne's name was all over the front pages of the tabloids for reasons that had nothing to do with football. The newspapers came out with a story of how when he was sixteen, Wayne had been seeing prostitutes in a Liverpool massage parlour. As you can imagine, the press went haywire. It was a horrible time. We were living in our house in Formby and the press swarmed the place. It was terrible. There were reporters and photographers everywhere.

The day before the story broke, we'd been tipped off that it was going to appear. At the time my mum and dad were on holiday in Florida with my sister Rosie and my youngest brother Anthony, so when I found out I went straight to my Auntie Tracy and Uncle Shaun's. There was no one else I could go to see, or who I wanted to tell, and I drove straight down there. All these thoughts were racing through my head. How was I going to break the news to my mum and dad? How do you tell them that kind of thing? Then I was thinking I needed to let my nan and granddad know what was happening before the newspapers came out the next day. I didn't want them waking up in the morning and finding out that way. I was just so upset, my head was all over the place. In the end, I couldn't bring myself to call my mum and dad, and Tracy called them for me. She did the same with my nan and granddad.

As soon as my mum and dad found out they wanted to come straight back home from holiday in Florida. I know they wanted to be there for me, but I told them there was nothing they could do. All they'd be coming home to was a load of press sat outside their house, so in the end they stayed in America. For anyone to deal with that kind of thing is heartbreaking, but I was only eighteen years old. I was so young, and all of a sudden I was faced with something that I could never imagine happening to me or my family.

Not only was I upset but the whole experience was just plain weird. I didn't know how to think or how other people would react. I wasn't sure what I felt about Wayne, but then part of me hated the idea that there might be members of my family who were going to turn against him. Their natural instinct is to protect me, and seeing something like that in the newspapers was bound to spark a reaction. It must have been hard for Wayne's family as well, but I wasn't around them at the time so I didn't know how they felt. I'm sure they must have been just as upset.

I just remember how difficult it was for me telling all my family what was going on. My granddad was sick at the time; it wasn't serious but he was laid up in bed, which made things worse. For days I didn't want to see anyone. That's my abiding memory of that time straight after the newspapers came out. Days later there was a family get-together at my nan and grand-dad's pub and everyone was there. I drove across with Tracy but couldn't bring myself to get out of the car. I watched everyone go in, all my family, but I didn't want to face anyone.

'Where's Wayne now?' Tracy asked me. I'd been with her on my own for a few hours. I told her he was at our house in Formby. She asked, did I want him to come down to her and Shaun's place? I didn't know what I wanted. Tracy said I needed to talk to him, that I needed to sort things out. She was right, so I told Wayne to drive over to my Auntie Tracy's. He came over and that's how the two of us ended up staying there for two weeks working things out.

If things couldn't get any worse, while all this was happening, Wayne finally decided to move to Manchester United and that caused its own problems and anxieties. In terms of football fans, and everyone seems to be football fans in the two cities, Liverpool and Manchester have always been fierce rivals, so my nerves were shot. I didn't know how people were going to react to Wayne's transfer, or even how the family would react. Not that they would have anything against Wayne, but, like I say, Liverpool and Everton supporters are not Manchester United's biggest fans.

But while Wayne was going to work every day, I spent the days sitting indoors thinking the whole world was against me.

The reaction was exactly what I'd expected. There was graffiti all over the walls near my mum's house, things like 'Judas' written over the walls, and 'Rooney scum', and 'Die', horrible things that were really hard to take. When Wayne signed, his new manager, Sir Alex Ferguson, told us he would do the best for us and if we ever needed any help or anything we should ask him. Had nothing else happened that summer other than Wayne's move then I would have felt like we'd gone through enough. But we had to cope with being on the front and back pages, and everywhere else in between. It felt like everyone was against us.

The strangest thing is, and unless you've been through something like that I suppose it's hard to comprehend, but, to be honest, even though it was a horrible time it was also the best of times. We had all our clothes brought across and we just lived at Tracy and Shaun's. They didn't want us to leave and we didn't want to go either. The reality was that while it was an awful period for everyone, the support of our family made it so much more bearable and made us feel better. Looking back now, the people closest to us allowed us the time to build things up between us again.

Apart from our closest family, no one knew we were there. The press had no idea where we were. Wayne would go to training at Manchester United in the back of my Uncle Shaun's little white van, then drive back home in secret. They'd take a different route every day. The paparazzi didn't know how he was getting to training in the morning.

But while Wayne was going to work every day, I spent the days sitting indoors thinking the whole world was against me. We were eighteen, we had been together for nearly two years, and we were engaged to be married. Then the newspaper story came out and everything turned upside-down. What Wayne had done was totally wrong, but the newspapers made out as though everything had happened yesterday. The story was two years old by the time it came out. I had been sixteen when he'd been going to this massage parlour. I'd started going out with Wayne in the August and all this had happened over the Christmas period, maybe four or five months into our relationship. I can't say that it was even a proper relationship at that stage. We used to meet at the chippy or the cinema or somewhere. That's what it meant to go out with someone at that age. What he'd done was wrong, but what sixteen-year-old is truly serious about a relationship at that age?

We should have been left alone to sort things out for ourselves, but I know that's not the way things are.

All this was going through my head and the newspapers made it worse. You don't want to read or take any notice of what they're saying, but when the story is about you it's hard to ignore, and the more I read the more I became upset and annoyed. Not only was I angered by the timing and the way the story had been written but I was also disturbed over what the newspapers were saying about me.

The whole story was being put across as if it had happened the day before, and so everyone was thinking, 'Oh, she's with him and he's doing that behind her back.' They were even saying stupid stuff like how Wayne might have a disease, and how I should ask him to be checked out at the doctor's.

The truth is, and I've never said this before, at that time in our relationship I'd never even slept with Wayne. I was only sixteen and we weren't having that kind of relationship at that stage. Had the story come out in those first few months then I don't think anyone would have cared in the slightest about me. Nobody knew who I was then. The newspapers wouldn't have bothered, and the story wouldn't have had the same impact. Instead, after a couple of years of running pictures of me shopping, the newspapers finally felt they had something to really get their teeth into, and so they began these nasty features about me. Most of them centred around the accusation that I was staying with Wayne just for his money. What other reason could there be, they said.

Nothing's that simple. No one's relationship is that straightforward. Me and Wayne had been together for two years and we were engaged. What Wayne had done in the past was wrong, but he knew that and he was sorry for what had happened.

So why did I stay with him? On the first night, when we sat

there in Tracy and Shaun's front room, I didn't know if I wanted to be with Wayne or not. I told him I didn't know what I wanted to do, or whether we should keep the relationship going. All Wayne kept repeating was how sorry he was. Everything wasn't all right straight away. It didn't work like that. But I knew that if there was a chance of us working things out then trust would have to be rebuilt over time.

Shaun and Tracy got us talking again, and after a few days of us hiding away in their house they said we should stop sitting around and go out. One day we went to Manchester shopping. There were no photographers around because no one knew we were going there, as nobody knew where we were. On another day we went to Blackpool Pleasure Beach, both of us with our hats on and our collars turned up. A few people recognized us but thankfully not any paparazzi. Again, it was just us two together, a young couple going out, without the paparazzi in tow, just as it had been in the very beginning.

Over that time, things became clearer in my head, and I realized that we would try to make things work between us. Gradually we started rebuilding our relationship. As I said, it's not a matter of one day waking up and saying, 'I'm going to stay with you.'

It was a horrible thing that had happened, though people do much worse. However, to have your personal life splashed all over the newspapers, to have the whole world discussing the private details of your existence, what you should and shouldn't do, writing about who you are when none of them know you, and blowing things out of all proportion, is an awful thing to experience. We should have been left alone to sort things out for ourselves, but I know that's not the way things are. That's not the way things will ever be again, I suppose. Our private life has become public property.

The overall effect on me as a person was that I lost a lot of my usual confidence. I'm normally a happy and out-going person, but back then it felt like some of that had been taken away. I was only eighteen years old, and I wonder if the journalists who wrote all those terrible stories really appreciated that. I doubt it, and I definitely didn't think so at the time. I hated the newspapers and I hated the media. I simply lost all my confidence and never wanted to speak to a journalist ever again. I didn't want the question of what had happened to come up, and I didn't want to put myself in the position of having to explain my life to a stranger, because I knew that's all anyone would want to talk to me about.

For a long, long time the newspapers and magazines made approaches to our manager, Paul, about doing interviews, and I would say I wasn't interested. When *Vogue* made a request, I didn't even think about who they were, I just thought about the prospect of doing an interview and said no, so Paul turned them down. It was then that Alexandra Shulman, *Vogue*'s editor, called again and promised that they weren't looking to do a hatchet job and they were interested from a purely fashion angle. So Paul came back to me and I thought that if I ever wanted to start doing things related to the media again then *Vogue* was the best road to go down. I told my mum and she was really pleased, but she also asked whether it was something I really wanted to do. I said yes.

I'm glad I decided to do *Vogue*. I'd done a few newspaper photo-shoots before, but when you work with a magazine like *Vogue* everyone on the team, from the photographer to the fashion editor to the make-up artist, wants to make the best possible photographs they can.

We shot the photos in an old house in Clapham, London, and I took my mum and Auntie Tracy down for support. When *Vogue* came out, the photographs looked great. As I've said before, it's one of my favourite shoots. It was also quite a turning point in my relationship with the press.

After *Vogue*, the newspapers suddenly began to write more positive stories about me, my style and my fashion, and, in the long run, allowed me to have the career I enjoy now. With regard to the press, I'd had to endure a steep learning curve, but I'd come out the other side and learned a lot about myself and other people, and the experiences made me a stronger person.

I am comfortable with the media now and like to think I have a good relationship with them. However, it is a relationship that is on a constant learning curve. On some days they'll come up with silly or annoying stories, but then on other days they write really lovely stories about me. It's true you can't always win, you have to take the rough with the smooth, the good with the bad.

Looking back, I went through some extremely difficult times, with things that you don't necessarily want to be seen up for public scrutiny. It was hard, and I know lots of people go through far more difficult times but that doesn't make your own problems any easier to cope with.

At such a young age I hadn't experienced anything like it previously. Fortunately I had the strength of character to come out on the other side and I also had the love and support of family and friends, people who were there for me. I will always be grateful to them – they helped get the normal Coleen back.

chapter seven

big betty, bob and doing a klinsmann: growing up a mcloughlin

Whenever I think about my childhood I've only got lovely, warm memories of a happy, busy family home in Croxteth. There was always somebody visiting or something going on, and that's just how I like to live now. If ever my brothers or I moaned about being bored our dad would always say, 'You're not bored. You can't be bored. There's no such word as bored.' And it's true. There's always something you can be doing.

I was four years old when we moved to Croxteth and I can't think of anywhere else I'd like to have grown up. It really annoys me when people describe it as a hard or a run-down area. There was a piece in a newspaper once that reported me as saying all you could ever hear in Croxteth was the sound of police helicopters flying overhead. I'd never say that. Croxteth is just the same as anywhere else: there are areas there that are a bit rougher than others, and some that are nicer. It's just normal.

Maybe it's because of his background as an amateur boxer, but my dad was the stricter one, whereas my mum has always been a bit more lenient. When I say strict, it wasn't in a nasty way. It's just that my dad loves to give you a talk. He'll sit you down and talk to you for ages – not only on how you should behave or the ways of the world, it could be any subject you care to mention. Growing up, we always sat down for dinner together as a family and ate at the same table and chatted about our days or listened to one of dad's 'talks'. We'd all moan sometimes but we knew he meant well.

There's that school uniform style again. With my brother Joe.

Nowadays, there are not enough families who sit down together for their dinners. It's almost like it's old-fashioned. But what it does do is make you more of a family. We've always been taught to appreciate each other, and although we never had a ton of money we knew from an early age to be grateful for what we had.

Ever since I can remember, Dad did and still does make a big thing of people saying 'please' and 'thank you'. If I take the family out for a meal, my dad will always say, 'Thanks, Coleen, that was lovely,' and he'll make sure my brothers do the same. Even if it's something small, like when we've all gone for a McDonald's and Wayne's paid, my dad will ask my brothers, 'Have you said thank you to Wayne for that?' Wayne used to find it funny because Joe and Anthony would come up after having had a cheeseburger and mumble, 'Thanks for that, Wayne.' Wayne would laugh his head off because he knew my dad had been on at my brothers to say their thank-yous. But my dad is right.

Bad manners are one of my pet hates. Good manners are just about being polite and appreciating other people, and having basic values that go towards making the world a better place.

As a family, we've always been brought up to respect other people as well as each other. Sure, we all used to fight as kids, but we were never serious. Because my dad was a boxer the house was always full of gloves and pads, so we used to mess about, giving each other 'boxer' names and having a fight. I was called

Big Betty, Joe was Little Josie, and I can't remember what our Anthony was but he must have been given a name. Joe and Anthony used to go training with my dad but I would have a good go. We'd fight, but it was just messing. I've always got on well with my brothers. Until recently, for as long as I can remember, whenever it was any of our birthdays, Mum and Dad would make us give each of the other two a five-pound note out of our birthday money. Later on it went from a fiver to a tenner. I used to moan sometimes but it's a really nice idea.

I'll have an argument but I've never been one to punch anyone. Actually, I've only ever had one fight in my life. It was during school lunch-break, people were playing football and this girl from another class wouldn't move out of the goalmouth. I don't know who started it but we were pushing each other at first, then we started pulling each other's hair. I remember the dinner ladies breaking it up and I was stood there with a clump of this girl's hair in my hand! The other girl had scratches on her face so the dinner lady was going to send her to the medical room. But first she said, 'You'll have to go to the headmaster's office.' I was always good at school so I started crying! The dinner lady walked with us to see the head and I cried all the way. Then, just before we reached the office, the dinner lady said that because neither of us had caused any trouble before she was going to let us off with a warning. I've never been so relieved in my life!

If I'm thinking about the happiest times I had as a child then Christmas has always been special. Like most kids, none of us could ever sleep, except at our house we'd be opening our presents and riding our new bikes up and down the street at three o'clock in the morning! When you get up that early it's really exciting

Big Betty, Bob and doing a Klinsmann

because then you keep looking out the window to see who else in the street has their lights turned on. 'So-and-so's up and they'll be opening their presents now,' I'd tell anyone who was listening.

Each Christmas-time we'd always get a new outfit. We were meant to save it until the actual holidays but, typically of me, I couldn't wait. Throughout the weeks leading up to Christmas Day, I'd come home from school and think, 'Ooh, I'll just try my Christmas clothes on.' Every tea time I'd stand in front of the mirror in my new outfit, admire myself, then neatly put everything away, all back on hangers, shoes back in the box. I'd go through exactly the same routine the next day! For weeks! My favourite outfit ever was a red and tartan skirt, a navy blue polo-neck jumper, navy tights and a red bubble jacket. The whole outfit was from Benetton.

An early taste of the spotlight in the school play with my friend Lisa. Love the hat!

I used to love Benetton when I was younger and my mum and Auntie Tracy went to Chester and Liverpool before she finally managed to find the skirt I wanted in Southport. I was so made up.

We'd actually get to wear our new outfits on Christmas Day morning when we went to church. Afterwards we used to fill the boot of the car with bin bags full of presents and drive around all the family giving them out, which used to take all day. I do love the Christmas period, but Christmas Day is one time that's not the same as you grow older.

Christmas-time and doing a 'Klinsmann' in the field behind our house are the two memories that will always remind me of growing up.

There always seemed to be more boys than girls in our area when we were kids, and my friend Amy-Louise and I would join my brothers and the other lads for a game of rounders at the back of our house. When it rained the field used to turn into a swamp, and there'd be loads of us, taking a run-up, then sliding and sliding through the mud, doing a Klinsmann. Jürgen Klinsmann, for any one who doesn't have to follow football as much as I do, used to be a German footballer, and he managed his national side during the 2006 World Cup. However, he was known over here for diving in the penalty area. After he joined Tottenham Hotspur that's how he used to celebrate his goals – by throwing himself forward and diving along the ground. That's what we used to do in 'the swamp', all of us arriving home covered in mud. And not only in the swamp, but by the paddling pool we had every summer in our back garden. I say paddling pool, but it got bigger and bigger every year. We'd all be in it, my dad and everyone. The grass would get soggy so we used to cover it with a blue plastic sheet. Then there'd be no excuse, and we'd be off doing the Klinsmann again. We've got videos of us at home all sliding along, making sure we hold our arms out in front to stop us from going headfirst into the concrete wall at the back of the garden. It was quite dangerous when I think about it, but no one got injured.

Touch wood, I've never broken anything. Apart from being in hospital when I was younger, I've only had two major injuries to speak of. One was when I was about eight, when I slipped while riding my bike around the garden and the bike's metal

With my nan and grandad.

Coleen: welcome to my world

stand sliced the back of my ankle. Blood poured out and I was taken to the hospital for stitches. I've still got the scar.

Two years earlier, I'd ended up in hospital again, for something a little more serious. It was New Year's Day and I was upstairs at my nan and granddad's pub, lying in front of the telly watching *Beetlejuice,* when their Alsatian, Shep, just turned around and bit me on the eye. My mum's not one to panic, but my nan couldn't help herself, and she thought Shep had bitten my actual eyeball. We rushed to the hospital and, luckily, it turned out the damage was just to the side of my eye, and for the next few weeks I walked around with an eye-patch. Shep was normally a lovely dog, so none of us knew what made him turn on me like that.

One of the things people always ask me is how we coped as a family when my mum and dad started fostering children, and particularly when we adopted Rosie. I can honestly say it never felt like a major difference. Our house in Croxteth has always been full and busy, the Frith family house, which is my mum's maiden name. It first belonged to Granddad and Nan Frith, then, long before I was born, Nan died, and Granddad, who we always called Bob, lived there alone. After that, when Bob eventually moved out with his new girlfriend, we all moved in.

But Bob was never away for long and was forever being bin-bagged, i.e. being turfed out by his girlfriend, and coming back to live with us. A former boxer, we always knew when he was back because so was his old exercise bike! We used to have a laugh with Bob but he was quite independent. I wasn't yet in my teens when he finally arrived back to live with us for good, and by then he was almost eighty years old. The one thing I always remember about him was that he had the only bedroom with a full-length mirror.

Once, when I thought he was asleep, I skipped in wearing nothing but my top and knickers, wanting to use the mirror. He went, 'Ohhh! Gerrout!' 'I'm just lookin'!' I said. After that, whenever I'd bolt into his room to use the mirror, he'd say the same thing: 'Ohhh! Just lookin', are you?'

I was about fourteen when he slipped on the bathroom tiles and died of a heart attack while in hospital. Even though he was in his eighties, it was a shock for everyone, but especially for my mum, who'd lost her mother when she was only sixteen years old. At his funeral, Joe, Anthony and I wrote poems on the service sheet, and I wrote 'Just lookin', Granddad!' at the bottom. Whenever I see a full-length mirror that phrase always pops into my head.

Our house was everybody's house. When my mum and dad started fostering, nothing changed for us, except we had someone new around. Rosie was no different at the beginning, except Rosie stayed and we adopted her.

Having someone in your family who suffers with severe disabilities doesn't change you as such. First and foremost, Rosie is my sister and I love her to bits. We would all have loved it if she had been born without Rett syndrome, and was not in a wheelchair, or fed through a tube in her stomach. But Rosie wouldn't be our Rosie if she was any other way. It's only when she's sick that you start thinking how lucky you are to be healthy. If Rosie's ill and she's crying, she can't tell you what's wrong with her because she can't talk. She can't tell you if she has earache or her stomach's hurting, and to see her go through those periods of illness is difficult.

There are times when I think it's not fair. For example, I hate eating in front of her. When she was younger she used to be able to eat in the same way as us, and Mum would mash up everything we were having. But now, because the condition of her throat and chest has deteriorated, she has to be fed by a tube that goes into her stomach. I don't think it's fair for her to have to watch me having my dinner, so I might go and eat somewhere else or put her in front of the telly.

Rosie loves watching DVDs – *Sesame Street*, *The Tweenies* and *The Fun Song Factory* are her favourites. Everyone in the house knows all the words to the songs as they get played over and over again! That's her excitement. She has got a lot wrong with her, but she's happy, and when you take her to hospital you appreciate that there are a lot of other people who are worse off. We can only do the best we can for her.

Together with Rosie and my cousin Sophia at Eurodisney, 2006.

We're still the same family now as before all the fashion shoots, the paparazzi, etc., and my family life is exactly as it's always been. You read about other people who've received the same press attention as me and Wayne, who have come into money, and how it can tear families apart, but that's not happened, and nor will it.

I never expected my life to be like it is now, so I'm sure my mum and dad feel the same, but they've never let it affect them. They've had the press camped outside their door, people have vandalized the house, written nasty graffiti on the walls, yet they've remained as solid and level-headed and as happy as they've always been. When something bad has been written, they're the first ones to say, 'Forget it, Coleen. They don't know

Meet the McLoughlins. With Mum, brothers Joe and Anthony and Dad before going to my cousin Colin and Emma's wedding.

you.' Like they've always said, I've got nothing to hide. I come from a normal family, where nobody has got anything to be ashamed of.

Earning the kind of money I do now, I instinctively want to give my family as much as possible, and it is great to buy them nice things. But they have never asked for or expected anything. When I bought them a new house it took ages before they finally chose to move away from Croxteth. They loved that area, but in the end they decided they would like a bit more space and privacy.

I help as much as I can, while at the same time respecting the fact that they are my mum and dad, and they want to live their life their own way. They don't want me buying them things all the time. Me and Wayne once tried to get my dad a new car for Rosie, a big Mercedes with wheelchair access. We had it on order but Dad said no, he didn't want it.

He said he had a car and as long as it had four wheels it was good enough to drive them round. My mum and dad are proud of what I'm doing, but I'm also aware that they're proud people as well.

All you ever want from a family is for them to be there for you, and that's how we treat each other. My circumstances might have changed, but my mum and dad haven't, my brothers haven't, and neither has the rest of my family. Whether it's been a school play, an exam or doing a TV advert, I've had their support from the very beginning.

None of us could have ever imagined the way things have altered over the last few years. There's been good and there's been bad, but this is our life now and it's something we've got to accept and not think about too much. What people write about us or say about us matters little in the end, as long as we get on with life just as we did before.

chapter eight

welcome to the world of colly mac

My mates mean everything to me. It says a lot about them that, never mind what's happened over the past few years, they've always been there, the same as ever, all of us up for a laugh, a few drinks and the odd heart-to-heart. Hopefully I've been there for them too. I hate to make a list of my friends, just because I don't want to miss anyone out. So, in case I do, I'm saying a big sorry now. I've got mates from St John Bosco High School for Girls, and a different gang from around where I used to live in Croxteth. I'll see them both together and separately, some often and some not as often as I'd like, but whenever we do get together for a girly night out, or for a birthday, or even, these days, for someone's engagement, it's just the same as it ever was, and that's the best thing you can ever say about a bunch of mates.

Before I start this chapter I want to name-check a few people. You might want to skip to the next paragraph or so because these names won't mean a lot to you, but they mean everything to me. So ... hello to Laura Knibb, Nadine Morris, Laura 'Chopper' Walters, Katie Garrity and her sister Christina, Danielle Lyons (funny one), Danielle Kelly (the first one of our friends to settle down with her boyfriend), Kelly Grogan (Midge), Kirsty Anderson, Kate

Ashort, Laura Holden, Victoria 'Plum' Matthews, Terri Ryan, Anita and Toni, Amy Louise from 'across the road', Jenna Hackett and Kate Wynn who were my best friends through school, the girls who I used to hang around in the Strand with: Rachel, Laura, Cara, Vicky, Michelle, Nicky, Leanne, Siobhan, Gemma, Catherine, Michelle, Jenny, Anne, Zoe and most of all my cousin Clair. Oh, and I forgot all my lad mates, but I would just keep going on and on. I am sorry again if I missed you out!

I'm big mates with all of the above, but now, because it's what happens when you get older and your life starts changing, the mates I see and speak to most on the phone these days are Claire Rooney (Wayne's cousin), Catherine Miller, Louise Brennan and Natalie Fenlan.

Just another low-key night out with the girls…

They've all got nicknames. Well, nearly all. They'll kill me if I say what they are, but, since I've got you wondering … Natalie Fenlan is 'Fen', which is fair enough, and Louise Brennan gets called 'Brenda'. We've been calling each other these names for so long that even our mums ask after everyone by their nicknames. Brenda gets a big cob on when we call her that, because now people actually think it's her real name and they'll say, 'Isn't that an old name for a girl of your age?' 'My name's Louise!' she's quick to come back. Catherine Miller gets called 'Cilla', as in Cilla Black. She hates that too. If other people start calling her Cilla she'll get a right cob on, worse than Brenda! Me? Well, Brenda sometimes calls me 'Colly' or 'Colly Mac', but that's not so bad. And Claire is just Claire, my best friend.

How can I best describe Claire? She's just like Wayne, dead laid back and really easy to be around. Claire has been through a lot with me. Our families have been friends since we were kids and we have known each other for years. She'll often travel down to London and keep me company on shoots or come with me to parties, and out of all my mates she's seen what it's really been like with the press, the photographers and all the attention.

You won't believe how comforting it is to have someone there who knows you inside out, who is looking out for you, and who is there to share what you are going through. It's really lovely to experience things through her eyes, to have a laugh with her and to just be normal girls in this crazy world that I sometimes live in. We were at Ashlee Simpson's after-show party on the night she'd made her West End debut in *Chicago*, and as soon as Claire sees Mum and Dad Simpson she's on the phone to our mate saying, 'Guess who's here?' I know it's not meant to be the thing to do in a cool London club, but that's exactly what I'm like sometimes.

It was great having Claire with me in Germany that summer during the World Cup. Normally, if there's a photographer snapping away she's not that keen to get in the shot so she'll stand behind me, but there was no way of avoiding the cameras over in Baden-Baden. Usually it's my mates looking at the newspapers saying to me, 'Look at your face there!', so it made a change to be able to do that with someone else. I remember going to the theme park in Germany and having a go on the water ride. The two of us were in the papers the next day and we just looked a total mess!

Life's a rollercoaster. Making a splash during the World Cup.

We were drenched, you could see all my extensions, and because my hair was soaked wet I looked half-bald ... Aghhh, we just looked like the worst scruffs ever.

There are other people who might get upset at having millions of people see you like that, but we're just two normal girls, acting our age, being real. And the pictures are funny, and funnier still when you've got your best mate sitting beside you!

Claire is always there for me. She'll go out of her way to do things for me. For example, if I'm going into town she might not want to come but she will because she knows how I much I hate being on my own when there's a photographer following me around. She's just a dead good mate. We speak on the phone every day, sometimes as much as five times, just to ask what each other's up to.

Brenda, Fen, Cilla ... all my mates are dead good, and since all this started I haven't seen a change in them at all. They are more aware of the life I'm leading, and they'll ask me about what I've been up to, but they're all the same people. There's no jealousy or envy because they've got their own lives. They haven't changed their fashions just because I have. They're not into clothes as much as me. If I come out wearing an expensive new dress, they just say, 'Oh, your dress is lovely,' but it doesn't matter to them whether it cost £10 from Asda or £1,000 from Cricket. Nothing like that bothers them. It's not in their nature to compete. They never have.

When the newspapers are nasty about me my friends take it personally, but otherwise they think it's funny to see me photographed all the time and they enjoy taking the mick. There have been loads of times when we've been around one or the other's houses having a laugh, and someone's said, 'Imagine if the press came in and saw us like this, they'd be made up!'

Last Christmas, Wayne bought one of those blow-up sumo-wrestler suits and we all had a go in it on Christmas Day. Not long after, a few of the girls were going round to Natalie's for a drink, and I brought it along and stashed it upstairs. Later on, after a few glasses of wine, I went up to the bedroom and came back down with this sumo suit on and we were in hysterics. Oh, we've got our use out of that suit! Well, I have. I was round at Natalie's not long ago, being Mrs Fat Sumo again, riding round the living room on her little brother's bike. The rest of them say, 'Imagine if the cameras were here now!' So much for the fashion phenomenon!

Together with best friend Claire at the *Closer* magazine party.

I love ridiculous things like that. Tell me a joke and I probably won't laugh because I don't find most jokes funny, but stupid things will send me and my friends into fits. I've got to admit, I'm a bit of a joker when I've had a drink. Natalie's mum has got a really fancy hoover that she once told us was dead expensive. Whenever we're all round there we're always skitting Natalie over this hoover, saying, 'Oooh, whatever you do, no one is to touch the hoover!' So one night, when we'd all had a little bit to drink, everyone decided to dress the hoover up! By the end it was wearing a cap, sunglasses, a jacket, everything … It was funny because we all know how much Natalie gets wound up about the hoover. But she laughed about it in the end. Silly things like that crack us all up.

Backstage chic at the 2006 V Festival in London.

Girly nights in usually involve us going round to someone's mum and dad's house, or they can come round to mine if they promise to behave themselves. It's never really anything special, just a load of us and a few bottles of wine. Every now and again we'll all have the facemasks on, doing a bit of a beauty treatment. If you take a moment out and sit back and listen, it's pure madness when we get going. There are a hundred conversations going on at once and everyone is shouting over each other. It's mad, but I enjoy those nights.

Girly nights out normally mean either going to a concert at the MEN in Manchester or a night out in Liverpool. That could be either a Friday night or a Saturday, but whichever it is the night will be planned a week in advance and we always go through the same routine.

A day at the races. With the girls at Aintree, 2006.

There might be as many as a dozen of us on a big night out, and in the days leading up we'll be on the phone to each other asking what everyone's going to be wearing.

Come the night, I might go round to Louise's or Katherine's house and we'll all get ready together. Sometimes I'll have my hair done at the hairdressers, go sort my things out round at my mum's then my dad or my brother will drive me over to my mate's house in my pyjamas, and I'll take my 'going out' clothes in a bag. We'll all have a drink, maybe a bottle of wine or a few vodkas, while we're all getting changed together. I don't really drink wine on a night out, I usually stick to vodka and Diet Coke.

We used to go to a local pub in Croxteth first before heading into Liverpool – usually the Lobster or Finnigans – but recently we'll get a taxi straight into town for about ten o'clock. Then it's on to a club.

I like to go somewhere like the Newz bar, because it's got private booths so you can sit and have a chat then maybe go on the dance floor if you fancy it. Or the Mosquito. Those are my favourites, but my mates all like going to mad clubs where it's packed, which if it's crammed and everyone is on top of each other can get a bit weary for me. I've not had any trouble for ages but I still get lads coming up to me having a go because Wayne left Everton to play for Man United. Everyone's drunk, so they'll come over and start shouting 'Your fella's a knobhead' or that I'm a slag. Nice. If it's a big nightclub, you might get the girls giving you little digs or sarcastic comments, but I laugh it off and put it down to jealousy. My mates like Claire and Louise will be the first ones to stick up for me, but I always tell them to leave it.

Pump up the volume

You're going for a night out with your mates and you need music to put you in the mood. Here are my top ten tunes to have you bouncing all over the furniture before the taxi arrives.

1. 'Crazy in Love' by Beyoncé. Still as good as the first time I heard it.

2. 'Fantasy' by Mariah Carey. Love this song.

3. 'Don't Cha' by The Pussycat Dolls. Shake your booty ... or something similar.

4. 'Red Dress' by the Sugababes. Just great pop.

5. 'Sexyback' by Justin Timberlake. Just Justin!

6. 'Touch the Sky' by Kanye West. I like the original 'Move On Up' by Curtis Mayfield but this is just as good.

7. 'Dirrty' by Christina Aguilera. This is brilliant. If this doesn't get you thrusting those hips then nothing will!

8. 'I Don't Feel Like Dancin'' by Scissor Sisters. What did we do before the Scissor Sisters arrived on the scene? Great disco with some great tunes. I could have chosen loads of their songs.

9. 'Get Right' by Jennifer Lopez. She's got the right curves and so has her music.

10. 'Bonnie and Clyde' by Beyoncé (featuring Jay-Z). I can't get enough Beyoncé.

I'm happy with my life, and if you react to the barrackers then they love it, because that's what they want.

To be honest, you only get that kind of thing once in a blue moon, and now it's nothing compared to when Wayne first switched clubs. I love Liverpool and I love going out there, and I think the people are great. Only a minority still bear a grudge. People have come to realize that I'm just this normal girl from Liverpool out for a good night with her mates. I'd hate to think other people would stop me going out and enjoying myself like I've always done.

Come 3 a.m., we're taxiing home, rolling back to my mate's at 4 a.m. in the morning and crashing out. I'll always make sure to

My best style pal. Together with Justine from Cricket [far left] at the Liverpool Awards.

Coleen: welcome to my world

The day after the night before

So you've had a good night and now you've woken up! And the sun is very, very bright outside. You might not want to leave your bed but, then again, you might have to. Try my guide to recuperation and you might just – I said just – feel like facing the world.

Open those eyes

A few eye drops will soothe bloodshot eyes so they look whiter and healthier again.

Be cool

Soothe puffy eyes with a cooling eye mask. For a homemade remedy try teabags or slices of cucumber. They do work!

Bring yourself to life

Use a radiance-boosting fluid or cream to rehydrate the skin, to get rid of the dull and to inject some glow.

Drink lots of water

It's been said before but it's worth repeating. Headaches and dull skin are caused by dehydration. Up your water intake and see the results.

Juice booster

Okay, your stomach is thinking McDonald's or KFC? But your head is pleading with you to go for something a little healthier. If you can suppress those junk-food cravings and you are able to drag yourself to the supermarket and then back to the kitchen, you'll feel the benefit of these power-boosting energy drinks. I can guarantee it.

Tropical Shake

You'll need: One mango (peeled and pitted), two oranges (peeled), half a papaya (seeded and sliced) and one banana (peeled).

All you have to do is: Juice the mango, oranges and papaya. Pour the juice into a blender, throw in the banana and liquefy.

Sunburst Smoothie

You'll need: One large orange (peeled), one sweet red apple and two cups of fresh strawberries.

All you have to do is: Put the orange into your juicer first, then add the apple and strawberries, pour into a glass and stir.

take a bottle of water to bed with me, though I'm still likely to get the odd hangover, in which case I'll have a couple of Nurofen and all diets go out of the window.

Whether it's McDonald's or KFC, I always eat junk food after a big night. It's not really a hangover cure but I can't seem to help myself!

I never want to lose touch with the mates I've got now. If there's one thing I miss about school then it's being around friends all the time. There's nothing like the mates you've grown up with, but as you get older you know it's not always possible to live the same life as you did when you were younger. Some friends of mine have babies now, so people's lives are changing all the time. The important thing is to make the most of the nights you do meet up.

I think that's where girls are better at keeping in touch than lads. Boys aren't on the phone all the time or texting each other the way we do. Wayne's lost some close friends along the way, mainly because he's constantly training or playing and he can't go out as much any more. When he was younger he might have gone out to clubs, but now he's more focused on his career. His job has meant that while he has lost friends along the way he has always been able to enjoy good friendships at the clubs he has played for. Unfortunately, it just means he doesn't get to hang around with the lads from Croxteth as much as he would like. Sometimes you grow up and you grow apart. One of Wayne's good friends now is my Uncle Shaun. Shaun's older than Wayne, in his mid-thirties. Shaun and Wayne will go out together, and Wayne has become friends with Shaun's mates. I think he feels he can trust them, and that's a big thing.

Every one of my mates has had newspapers offering them money for stories about me. The press now know that no one is going to speak to them, not any of my real friends, but in the past journalists would walk around Croxteth asking people where Coleen's friends lived. It's mad the way the press get addresses and telephone numbers and just pass them around. All my mates have had letters shoved through the door, trying to sweet-talk them round with offers of money, makeovers, all sorts. Claire has been asked loads of times to sell her story, but none of my real friends have ever spoken to the newspapers about me.

I've only had one girl I know from school come out and say something that's become a story in the newspapers. That was when they published a page out of my old school yearbook from St John Bosco's, in which we'd all been asked to write where we'd like to be in ten years' time. I'd written that I wanted 'to be famous, living a life of luxury'. The girl who went to the newspapers was in my year but she was never a close mate. We were sixteen when I wrote that. It was coming to the end of term and our form teacher passed the yearbook round and told us to make a joke out of it, and just to put what we'd love to do. What I hated about the way the story came out in the press was how it made me look like this conniving, fame-hungry person who would do whatever it took to get where I wanted to be. That wasn't the case at all. All the girls in my Performing Arts class wrote similar things, like how they wanted to be living on a desert island dripping in diamonds. I've got that yearbook, and some girls wrote normal stuff about wanting to run their own businesses or be police officers, but because I was studying Performing Arts and that's what I wanted to do then it was just natural to wish to become a famous actress. It was just kid's talk. The newspapers made a big thing out of it, as if to say, 'Well, she's got what she wanted ...' in a nasty way.

I would never say I wanted to be famous. I'd say 'I want to be a successful actress,' but famous is not a word I would use again. I didn't know what being famous meant at the time. Now it's come to mean people who'll do anything to get their names in the papers. That's not me.

So if you ever see the words 'Coleen McLoughlin' and 'a close friend says' in the same newspaper story you can take my word for it that there's not an ounce of truth there. My close mates are proper mates, and they would never sell out for a few quid. We've all grown up together and we're going to go on growing up together. They've always been there for me and I'm always going to be there for them.

chapter nine

food and fitness: it's like my dad has always said…

Every magazine or newspaper you pick up these days seems to be obsessed with how skinny or fat female celebrities are. I'm a big fan of the fashion of Nicole Richie and Lindsay Lohan, but I'm aware that they've come in for more than their fair share of criticism in recent times. I find it hard to comment on the weight of another girl unless I know her, but if they want to be that thin then fair enough. Obviously, that doesn't mean I promote starving yourself to death to achieve what you think is your ideal shape, but I think that if you eat healthily and exercise then it's up to you how you look. I don't know about Nicole Richie and Lindsay Lohan, but the truth is that there are girls out there who are naturally thin. I've got friends who can just eat and eat whatever they want and stay the same shape. That's their metabolism, although maybe that will change for them over the years.

Unfortunately, like most girls, I'm the total opposite. If I eat and eat and eat then, guess what, I put weight on! So, sometimes I'll cut down a little and maybe exercise a bit more, and hey presto, I'll lose a few pounds. I'm a normal girl! But if you believe what you read in the magazines and newspapers then you'd think I was some yo-yo dieter, not in control of my body. One week they'll have me down as this 'chubby so-and-so', and the next they'll be praising me for the shape I'm in.

I do think all these stories put pressure on girls, whether they are celebrities or not, and having experienced that kind of scrutiny myself I can understand how, if you let them get to you, you're likely to take the criticism personally and it will affect you. My view is that as long as you are happy with your own shape then that's all that matters. You can't let others determine how much you should weigh and what you should wear. The fact is that there are some fashions that look better on a slimmer figure, but like I've always said, 'I'm me, and I'll wear what I like, and what I think I look good in.'

My view is that as long as you are happy with your own shape then that's all that matters. You can't let others determine how much you should weigh and what you should wear.

When the press go on about my weight, I ignore them. I know for a fact I've never been fat, so when they criticize me I don't take any notice. While we were on holiday after the World Cup, they were asking whether I was pregnant. No, I wasn't! I'd just put on a few pounds and they happened to take a picture of me with my belly sticking out. It's not the kind of photo you'd keep for the family album, but every girl knows the unflattering beach look. Likewise, when they said I'd lost some weight the truth was that it wasn't all that dramatic a change. It was simply that I'd stepped up my gym programme in preparation to make my fitness DVD and so I had toned up a bit.

The last people I'd take notice of would be those writing in newspapers. I'm surrounded by family and close friends who'll tell me their opinion if they think I've put a bit of weight on. Those are the people whose opinion I trust. If I turn to my eldest brother Joe, I know he'll be honest with me. I asked him recently whether I'd got bigger and he said, 'Yeah, you looked like a stump when you were walking the other day!' And, to be honest, I know that sometimes when I wear jeans and flat shoes I can look a bit stumpy. We can't all be blessed with long legs like Giselle! Maybe 'stumpy' was going a bit too far, but I listen to the people that are close to me.

I'm not and never have been one for fad diets. That's why I used to go to Weight Watchers with my mum. A while ago the newspapers made a big thing about me being spotted going to the local slimming club near where my mum lives, as if it was something to be ashamed about. Under normal circumstances I wouldn't give people the privilege of a response to something like that, but in my column in *Closer* I made a point of bringing the subject up. No one should be made to feel embarrassed about joining a club like Weight Watchers, and if me talking about the subject helps a girl who is upset with their weight then I don't mind.

Weight Watchers isn't a bad diet, it's not to do with starving yourself. Every now and again I'll go with my mum to the local church club at Queen Martyrs in Croxteth. I prefer to go to a place where I'm surrounded by people I know, and down there it's full of neighbours and friends I used to go to school with. I just feel more comfortable doing that kind of thing with people I've grown up with and known all my life. Sometimes I'll go to the local sports centre and join a class. The last one I took was a body-combat class. Someone who I hadn't seen for ages happened to be in the class and said, 'Oh, why are you going round by ours? I'd rather go where you don't know anyone.' I just don't feel that way, and that's why I'll go to the local Weight Watchers with my mum and her mate and not some exclusive fitness club. I like it there. Simple as that.

I prefer a slimming diet that allows you to eat normal food as long as you don't overindulge. Not that I'm dieting all the time. It's only recently that we've had a set of scales in the house and that's because Wayne decided to buy some so he could keep track of his own weight. I sometimes use them but I'm not obsessed. I believe it's what you feel inside that counts, not what's on the scales. Instead, I'll rely on how I feel about myself, or how I feel inside my clothes, and then, if I think I need to, I'll will lose a little weight and step up my exercise. I can't stand those diets that say you can't eat this and that.

like my dad says, a little bit of everything is always good for you

Because my dad used to be a boxer when he was younger he always had a balanced diet, and that used to affect the way we ate when we were kids. In the kitchen he'd have a piece of paper stuck to the fridge or pinned on a cupboard door and it would list all the food for the week that would give him a balanced diet. So, for example, on a Monday he'd make sure he had beans, and this would go on right through to Sunday, when sardines were on the menu – the idea being that he evened out all his carbs and his proteins and his vitamins. I have cousins and friends who could eat whatever they wanted growing up, and they'd have different meals cooked specially for them, but my mum would use the list, cook us all the same meal and we'd be made to eat it. Made to eat it! That sounds a bit strong. None us ever complained, except when it was liver on a Wednesday, and Mum would do her best to hide the flavour with gravy or mint sauce, or serve it up with onions, sausage and mash. Fridays was always fish – it might be battered or something like cod with parsley sauce. And on Thursdays it was takeaway, which usually meant a trip to the chippy round the corner. Or the Chinese. I used to have boiled rice with barbecue sauce. That was it! A portion of boiled rice with barbecue sauce, and I used to love it. I haven't got much to complain about nowadays in terms of the beautiful home we have and the area where we live, but I do miss not having a local Chinese chippy! Looking back on growing up, I can't moan about my dad's lists or the food we had every night. Joe, Anthony and I might have had a little moan at the time, but it was good for us in the long run. We're all healthy and I think it's good we weren't fed fish fingers, chips and beans or a takeaway every night.

All this talk of food is making me hungry! Because I really do like my food and that's one of the reasons I could never be on a diet all the time.

If me and Wayne are treating ourselves, our favourite meal out would be either a Chinese or an Italian. If it's a Chinese then we go to a restaurant in Manchester called Wings, where a lot of our friends go. We love it there and the people who run it are really lovely to us. We turned up one day and the manager said to Wayne, 'Do you like your chopsticks?' We said, 'We're happy with the

A recipe for getting into shape

I love food, but occasionally I feel the need to lose a few pounds.
Whatever diet or exercise regime I follow I always stick to these three
basic tips to see me through:

1. I'm not a big fan of weighing myself on scales

I always believe it's how you feel inside that counts. Muscle
really does weigh more than fat, so good exercise means that
while you may not be losing the pounds your body is becoming
more toned.

2. Buddy up

There's nothing lonelier than exercising or dieting on your own.
Team up with a friend or relative and encourage each other when
you're not in the mood. That's why me and Mum still visit the
slimming club together.

3. A little bit of naughty is nice ... and good for you

It's not healthy to be strict with yourself. Give your body a
holiday. Me and Wayne will have a Chinese or Italian (no cream
dishes, please) once a week, and I can't resist the odd bag of
cheese and onion crisps!

chopsticks, thanks.' 'No,' he said, looking down at the table, 'do you like the chopsticks?' We picked them up and they had our names written on the side. It was really sweet of them. The manager said that every time we came for dinner we'd have our own chopsticks. Wayne was made up. He loves things like that. He loves being the only one or the first to have something, like cars and gadgets. He couldn't wait for the next time he came down to Wings with the Man United lads and the waiter brought out his very own chopsticks!

Anyway, back to food. If it's Chinese then we'll start off with dim sum, or maybe spring rolls or char sui buns. If we go for starters then maybe we'll share a main between us. I like the filet of beef in black pepper sauce, but Wings do this sea bass in ginger with spring onions that is gorgeous, and it comes for two so we share. There are prawn crackers on the table already, but I try to avoid them as they are dead fattening. Drink-wise, it's usually Diet Coke, but if we're drinking alcohol then it's our favourite sauvignon blanc, by Cloudy Bay.

If we go Italian, then I'll usually have a soup starter, something like tomato and basil, or maybe some garlic bread with cheese. For main, I really like tomato-based pastas, so it might be bolognaise or penne with chicken and garlic. Wayne normally orders a salad for starters, and it's usually a Caesar salad. He'll go to a restaurant and he'll order a salad for a main course, whereas I just can't do that. I'm terrible. For my lunch, maybe I'd eat a salad, but not for my dinner, unless I'm on a strict diet. If I go out for a meal I see it as a treat, so I'll eat a steak or something. However, even round at my mum's Wayne will always ask for a salad, either on its own or with chicken.

I love going to my mum's to eat. She's a great cook. She'll do loads of different stuff – when we have family parties everyone asks my mum to do a big pan of chilli con carne – but my favourite is her spaghetti bolognaise. Wayne loves my mum's spaghetti bolognaise.

When it comes to dessert, I'm not really that bothered if I've had a big dinner. I've never really been into desserts. I know that's unusual for a girl, but I prefer a packet of crisps to a bar of chocolate. At Easter, when I was a kid, I always used to be given clothes instead of Easter eggs. I think that was my idea! I've never really liked chocolate and I still don't really eat it.

My downfall is that sometimes I'll go without breakfast. I know that's bad, but often I'm flitting between my house and my mum's house, sometimes going to a photo-shoot or attending a promotional event, and I'll just pick up something along the way. On an evening, if Wayne's not away with the club – in which case I'll stay over at my mum's – the two of us try to sit down to dinner together.

Unfortunately, I've not inherited my mum's love of cooking.

I mean, I'll have a go at doing different things like pasta or fish, or I'll make chicken bolognaise rather than use mince; but it doesn't matter how hard I try, my spaghetti bolognaise never seems to taste as good as mum's. So I normally keep to simple stuff like tuna steaks or stir-fries. Unfortunately, you'll never see me making a layered lasagne or anything like that.

Food and fitness: it's like my dad has always said…   **141**

So it's a good job that Wayne is easy to cook for because he likes salads so much. Wayne's not really one of those boys who spends too much time in the kitchen. If he's making toast or something he'll do a slice for me, but he's not one for putting the chef's hat on. Although there was one time, in our house in Formby, when he made steak, chips and sweetcorn, with peppercorn sauce over the steak. He told everyone he did it by himself, but I helped him really! With a little extra assistance from George Foreman's grill.

On an average week, I'll usually try to eat healthily from Monday to Friday, then it often goes downhill on a Friday night.

During the week I'll aim to have cereal for breakfast – Cornflakes or Sugar Puffs – with semi-skimmed milk. Then for lunch I'll have a salad or a sandwich, although I hate buying sandwiches because they put loads of rubbish in them. At Mum's maybe I'll have soup or spaghetti hoops, just on their own, warmed up. I like them. Then in the evening I'll try to have a proper meal with Wayne.

When it gets to Friday – well … it doesn't always go to pot but I'll often go round to my friends' houses and start picking at stuff. On the Saturday after a night out it's difficult to avoid eating rubbish once you have woken up. If I'm out shopping with mates in Liverpool on the Saturday then we might pick up a butty or a McDonald's on the way home. I've got to admit that I can't resist the taste of McDonald's. I think my cravings date back to when I was a kid and my favourite game was playing 'shop' with this massive toy drive-through McDonald's. It was great. It made all the noises for grilling the burgers and frying the chips, then you'd have your little Happy Meals and all the food in plastic. Mum's still got it now, somewhere up in the loft. She says she wants to keep it in case she has grandchildren!

When the time comes for a healthy regime, I'll change my food habits and pick up on the exercise. For starters I'll make sure that I always have breakfast. I know everyone says it's the most important meal of the day, but I'm not very good at eating first thing without making a real effort. When I began training for my fitness DVD I started having porridge in the morning with a few raspberries. I don't like it that much but it made me feel more awake for the rest of the day. As part of being healthy I'll go on the slimming plan and start counting and writing everything down, then I'll try to go to the gym at least three times a week.

I used to go to the local sports club but now we're lucky enough to have a gym in our new house, with all the machines and weights, and I have a personal trainer, Elise Lindsay, who'll come round to the house maybe two or three times a week. She's really good fun and I think I need that, to have a laugh with her. The two of us got together just before I made my fitness DVD and I've stayed with her ever since. I enjoy her company, which is good. I know some people want their trainers to be mean to them, but I don't. I want the sessions to be enjoyable ... and to do them in the mornings, because then it's over and done with!

Usually, Elise will vary the sessions. One day we might do core work like Pilates, then the next we'll base it more on the cardio area, then the day after we'll maybe work a bit more with the free weights. An average session consists of a ten-minute

Get fit quick

If you're looking to get into shape then it's always best to join a gym or a class. I use the gym two or three times a week, but if I want a quick 45-minute workout to perk me up I'll do the following (remember, if you're not used to regular exercise you should always consult your doctor first):

Stretch those muscles and loosen up with a 5-minute walk.

Take your pick. This is your 25-minute aerobic workout. Either jump on your bike, pull on your running shoes or get the skipping rope out. For variation you can do a bit of all three, as long as you hit the 25-minute mark.

Step it up. Stand at the foot of your stairs. Take a step up, putting your right foot first, then step down, again with your right foot first. Repeat 30 times, then switch to putting your left foot first.

Stride lunges. Great for your butt and thighs! Stand with your feet 8 inches apart, toes pointing ahead. Step two or three feet forward with your left leg, so your right knee is a few feet above the ground. Then return to your start position. Repeat 10 to 15 times, then switch to putting your right leg forward.

Hit the squat. Stand with your feet shoulder-width apart. Bend at the knees as though you're about to sit down. Once your thighs are parallel to the ground, slowly return to the start position. Repeat 10 to 15 times.

Front lift. Take two litre bottles of water. Keep the arms straight and slowly raise to shoulder height. Repeat 10 to 15 times.

Side lift. Exactly the same as the front lift, only this time the arms are raised to the side. Repeat 10 to 15 times.

Arm curls. Hold the water bottles straight out in front with palms facing up. Bend at the elbow, working those biceps, then return to your start position. Repeat 10 to 15 times.

Tummy crunch. Do 15 sit-ups. Rest. Then do another 15.

Tummy tightener. Lie on your stomach. Pull and contract your belly button towards your spine, hold, then release. Repeat 20 times.

Scissor leg lift. Lie on your side, resting on your elbow. Keeping your leg straight, lift towards the ceiling then slowly return to your start position. Repeat 15 times on either side.

Finally, stretch for a good few minutes.

warm-up on the treadmill or the cross-trainer, then another ten minutes on the rower and then the stepper for five minutes. We'll do some weights, then bench presses for my upper body, and finish off with some core work on the ball, like sit-ups.

My problem is that I hate running. They reckon running is probably the best exercise you can do to lose weight but I hate it. I'd love to say differently, but I just can't get to grips with my breathing, and when I run I get bored and out of breath dead easily, whereas I can do other things, like skipping or aerobics, for ages. Maybe I should try to go jogging outside. Me and Wayne always say we're going to buy a couple of bikes and go out cycling but we never get round to it. We've got a tennis court in the garden but we've only had a couple of games and I'm not very good at it. I'm determined to get better.

I know I'm engaged to a footballer but sport has never really been a big love of mine. At school I was more into Performing Arts and the drama club. The only sport I've ever been really good at is swimming, and that was when I was at junior school. By senior school I was less determined. Although I wouldn't describe myself as competitive I know that if I take part in something I want to win, but that doesn't mean I'm a bad loser. Even when I was entering the various sports competitions I was more interested in it being a good day out with mates than anything else. I'd have a go at everything at school. I was okay at sprinting, but not cross-country. Once I took part in the long jump, and to this day I don't know why because I really was very poor.

I suppose I'm like most girls really – I want to keep fit but I'm not obsessed. You might think I would be different because I'm with Wayne, but that's his job, to keep his body in shape.

When he was trying to get fit for the World Cup he'd come home from the club and do more training in the gym at home. That's the dedication of a professional athlete.

Me and Wayne always say we're going to buy a couple of bikes and go out cycling but we never get round to it.

The only time I've ever got close to knowing how he feels exercise-wise was when I was training to do my fitness video. We don't irritate each other much but the one thing Wayne does that gets on my nerves is when he comes back from training in the afternoon and either lies down in front of the telly or falls asleep. I just can't understand why people want to sleep away the day. I hate it, and I'll be on at him to wake up. But when I started doing my fitness DVD I'd come home knackered and all I'd want to do was rest. Wayne got his own back then. 'See,' he'd say, 'that's what I feel like when I come in from training!' Ever since then I've been a bit more understanding.

Like my dad has always said, 'Food and fitness ... it's all about balance.'

chapter ten

are they talking about me?

The funny thing about being in the world we're living in now is separating the fact from the fiction. Well, I've no trouble doing that, but it's not so easy for others. There have been countless times when my mum or an auntie has overheard someone saying they've heard Coleen has been doing this or that, and they'll try not to get involved but occasionally they'll feel the need to intervene. 'How do you know?' the girl will ask them. 'Well, I should know, because Coleen's my daughter,' my mum will reply.

It's the same with my nan. No matter how many times we've told her to stop believing what she reads in the newspapers she's forever ringing up asking whether what she's heard about 'Our Coleen' is true? No, Nan, I promise you, it's not!

Because both me and Wayne are in the newspapers most days, people think they know us and there is a certain part of us that becomes public property. We are aware that we wouldn't be here now if it wasn't for the fans and the media, and we do get people coming up in the street or a bar and striking up a conversation. Sometimes that's great because you often meet lovely and interesting people, but there are others who are just plain rude.

As I've already mentioned, I've got a big thing about manners. Sometimes people come up and say, 'Oh, Wayne, put your name on that. I don't support your team, but I'll have your autograph!' I often wonder why they want his autograph if they don't support him. I don't complain, but occasionally it gets a bit ridiculous. One time, we were flying back and the air steward kept bringing passengers up for autographs. We hate to refuse, especially when it's kids, but we'd been up since 4 a.m. and just wanted to watch a film or go to sleep. Towards the end I felt like I was going to flip. Then the steward came up again with two children saying they wanted my boyfriend's autograph. I told him Wayne was in the toilet, so he took the children towards the toilet, saying, 'C'mon, we'll wait outside.' I couldn't believe it!

As I say, it's not that we really mind, it's just that there are times when you want some privacy.

It wasn't long ago that Wayne was asking footballers for their autographs, so he knows what it feels like.

When he was ten or eleven he was a big fan of the Everton and Scotland striker Duncan Ferguson, who he went on to play with and who is now a friend. Duncan was Wayne's hero, and when Duncan spent time in prison for something that happened on the football pitch Wayne wrote to him in jail. I was never one for autographs or posters on my bedroom wall, even though I was always a fan of Take That, but nevertheless me and Wayne both know what it's like to be on the other side and so we do try to be as accommodating as possible.

This chapter isn't about autograph-hunters, though. It's about becoming public property, and how because people read about you in the newspapers every day they think they know you and your life. The stories that newspapers run more often than not affect how the public sees you and how they react towards you. Reality is usually very different, and the fallout from such rumours and lies not only affects my and Wayne's lives but also those of our families and friends. So I just want to go through a few stories that have been written about me in the past and explain what really happened, and I'll give you the whole truth and nothing but...

'Coleen the Smuggler — Rooney's Fiancée Held over £40,000 Spree'

In 2004 the newspapers reported that I'd been to New York on a shopping trip and, having spent £40,000 on designer labels, was hauled in by customs officers at Manchester Airport for walking through the 'Nothing to Declare' channel. After being interrogated by customs for three hours, it was said that I had to pay a 'whopping' £31,000 in duty and penalties. The *Daily Star* quoted a police source as saying that the wives and girlfriends of Premiership footballers were bringing goods back into the country and failing to pay duty. They said it was a scam conducted by the rich and famous.

I went to New York with my Auntie Tracy and Uncle Shaun and their mates. It was a few months after all the trouble with Wayne and they asked me if I wanted to come with them for a break. Before I'd even left England, the newspapers had printed a big picture of me on their front pages with the headline, 'Coleen Goes On £10,000 Shopping Spree in New York'. How did they know? I hadn't even been yet!

After five days in New York we arrived back home at five in the morning. I had been shopping while I was over there, but I hadn't spent nearly as much as they said. I'd just bought some bits of Juicy gear, iPods, and some stuff for Wayne. I honestly didn't know you had to declare it, I thought it was all duty free. Everything had price tags on so I wasn't trying to hide anything. Regardless, customs pulled me in, telling me, 'Did you know you can't spend over £145 without declaring?' and started going through my suitcases. The whole process took ages – I was in there for three hours – while they wrote the prices of everything down. In the end, I just tipped the bag out and said, 'I bought it all there!' Finally, after paying the tax on the goods I'd bought and a fine of about £2,000 I was allowed to leave the airport. Fair enough, but it did feel like customs were making an example of me, and having seen the £10,000 shopping-spree story they were ready and waiting for me when I came back home. I hadn't even left customs and the airport was swarming with reporters and TV crews – it was ridiculous. If that wasn't enough, not long after the incident these adverts began appearing in the business papers in the run-up to Christmas, saying, 'Christmas Shopping: Don't Do What Coleen Did'. So, without my permission, they ended up using my case as an example to highlight their campaign! Maybe in return they should have given me my fine back!

'Coleen Turns Pop Princess'

Apparently, according to the newspapers, I was going to become a
pop star. There was this woman, I think her name is Jennifer John,
who had taught Atomic Kitten, claiming that I'd been having
singing lessons with her and that I sounded like Delta Goodrem!
'Coleen loves singing and has recorded some tracks,' the paper
said. 'She has lots of time and money on her hands.'

I've never met the woman in my life and my voice is terrible.
I can't sing. I was in the choir at school but that was only because
I love drama and my dream was to be an actress, and you couldn't
take part in school productions unless you joined the choir. But
even in the choir I think I used to either speak the song or just
have my mouth opening and closing. I'm really no good at all. I'm
definitely no Delta Goodrem!

'Wayne Gets Coleen a Gang of Minders – Ace Fears She's a Kidnap Target'

A few years ago, this story appeared claiming Wayne had hired
minders to protect me from kidnappers, thieves and jealous girl
gangs in Liverpool when I was out on my own.

We've never had bodyguards. Occasionally, because of the
press attention, we'll have Steve with us for security. He's an ex-
policeman and works for our management company. In the past,
we've had someone on holiday with us, but never a big group.
I did a shoot for Asda in Portugal and they gave me four bodyguards, all dressed in black, all with shaved heads. They said they

shaved their heads so that if they were in a fight no one could pull their hair! They guarded me like I was the Queen, and when I sat down between shots they'd all come and stand around me so no one could get near. However, I just couldn't deal with that on a regular basis, twenty-four hours a day.

Obviously, security is a serious subject. Thankfully, we've never had any kidnap threats, but you do hear about them with other people and it could easily happen.

We try to live as normal a life as possible. Yes, we do occasionally get idiots saying stuff to us when we're out, but we just have to ignore it, otherwise we're allowing other people to mess up our lives. I do worry sometimes, thinking about the dangers, but you've simply got to be constantly aware of people and situations. My dad is always telling me to be careful if I go out, especially if I'm on my own. To be honest, whether it's out in town on a night, or out shopping, I'm never really on my own. I'm the kind of person who likes being with other people, so I'm usually with family or friends.

At the moment, fortunately, I don't need twenty-four-hour security, and I hope I never will.

'Roo Not Disturb – Two Days in Paris – and Wayne and Coleen Spend 36 Hours of It in a Hotel Bed'

This is the kind of story that would be funny if it wasn't plain embarrassing. Just before Christmas in 2004, the *Sun* ran a piece saying that we'd gone away for a break 'and celebrated [our] trip to Paris with a gigantic bonkathon'! According to them, we stuck a 'Do Not Disturb' sign outside the door of our £1,000-a-night suite, ordered room service of chicken nuggets and cheeseburgers, then when we finally emerged Wayne looked 'exhausted'!

It's all a load of rubbish. Wayne had a few days off, so we went to Paris for a couple of days and stayed in the beautiful George V Hotel – that much is true. But, no, we ate out most of the time, either in the hotel restaurant or once at the top of the Eiffel Tower, and we went sight-seeing, and took a boat trip down the Seine. I knew they'd sent a female reporter to stay at the hotel, so you'd think they'd get their facts right, but I suppose that doesn't make as good a story. In one newspaper they said I went down to dinner wearing a Burberry-style dress, playing on all that Chav rubbish. It was Missoni.

'As Rooney is disgraced again, read the latest gloriously tacky episode in the life of designer-loving, comfort-eating, bank-emptying, Merc-driving, jewellery-dripping, Wayne-forgiving … QUEEN COLEEN'

This was a feature that appeared in the *Daily Mail* and was written a few days after Wayne played for England in Spain and had made the headlines for storming off the pitch in frustration at being substituted. The article was more than 2,000 words and amounted to a nasty character assassination of not only me, but of my family and Wayne's. The personal attack ranged from snipy vindictiveness to the ridiculous. Among the slurs it quoted an unnamed 'contemporary' as saying, 'Coleen would have probably ended up working in a biscuit factory if she hadn't met Wayne.' The piece accused me of being a gold-digger and spending Wayne's money – 'Her motto seems to be if it's expensive, but not necessarily stylish, it's definitely worth buying,' and it said I'd gained over a stone in weight from 'comfort-eating'. It also reported that I had my own personal shopper at Harvey Nichols in Manchester, who supplied me with 'champagne and chit-chat about where to point [my] very exclusive credit card'. But worse still was that the journalist had a go at our families, and reported that our parents were supposedly involved in some kind of feud. Once again there was the story of the so called punch-up at my eighteenth birthday party at the Devonshire House Hotel, which I've recounted already in this book. It is one thing to have a go at me and Wayne but to bring our families into it is low. The story went on to say how during Euro 2004 in Portugal it was the McLoughlins who stayed in the official hotel for families and partners and not the Rooneys. Rubbish. Only me and my friend Laura stayed at the official hotel and my mum and dad only came to visit while they were over for a couple of matches. They even wrote a piece saying the 'McLoughlins are moving into Wayne and Coleen's palatial former home' while 'the Rooneys have been installed in a much smaller property in another part of Liverpool'. It was just petty, nasty, disgusting stuff.

The story was written by a journalist called Paul Bracchi and the morning I read it I was so furious that I picked up the telephone and rang the *Daily Mail* offices. I've never done anything like that before but I just couldn't sit there and do nothing. It took me about an hour, but eventually I was put through.

'Hiya,' I said.

'Hello.'

'Do you know me?'

'Sorry?' he replied.

'Do you know me?' I asked him again.

'No,' said Paul Bracchi.

'Well,' I said, keeping calm, 'if you don't know me, how come you can write a two-page spread about me and my family? You wrote two pages on me and my family, without knowing me or them, not knowing anything about us, and ninety-nine per cent of what you've written is a load of rubbish.'

I was on the telephone with him for an hour, telling him his 'sources' were rubbish and that if he was going to write about me again then at least he should find people who were going to tell the truth. I'd never rung up a newspaper about a story before, and I haven't since, but when someone had attacked us and our families like that I just couldn't stop myself, and I'm glad I did it.

'Dump the thug. Friends say bad boy Rooney must go after slap in nightclub'

This is one of those times when the newspapers just print pure evil lies about you. The incident happened several years ago and it was claimed that me and Wayne were out in a Manchester nightclub with friends when we started arguing. They wrote that Wayne pulled my hair, threw a drink over me and then slapped me. Another newspaper said he punched me in the ribs. We actually sued the *Sun* over this story and it was eventually settled out of court in our favour and the newspapers involved ran an apology. Again, a so-called 'friend' was quoted as saying, 'She's got to get rid of him – he's got no respect for her and treats her like dirt.' There were newspapers and TV programmes devoted to our relationship, featuring people from a wife-beaters' association commenting on our supposed situation.

The truth is, yes, we did have an argument that night in Brasingamens nightclub in Alderley Edge, but it wasn't a big shouting match. The music was so loud that I can't imagine anyone even noticing. I think the reason that people put two and two together and made five is that we hadn't been in the club long before we left. And there was a good reason for that. The next day I had to fly out to Cyprus at 4 a.m. to do a photo-shoot and that was part of the reason we were arguing, because I didn't want to stay out late as I had to get up early the next day. Also, it was simply a lovers' tiff. A few of us had been round to Rio Ferdinand's house earlier to watch a match but then the lads decided to go off to the pub to get something to eat and left us girls behind. They went out, so we decided to go out! When we met up in Brasingamens we had a bit of an argument. It was nothing and Wayne certainly didn't slap me.

'Coleen Buys Own Store'

According to the *Daily Star*, my friend Dawn Ward and I had splashed out £550,000 on a shop near my home in Cheshire and we were going to open a 'swanky boutique'. They even quoted the owner as saying that she was made an offer she couldn't refuse. I bet she couldn't! Judging by the photo in the newspaper it was only a tiny shop. I know I worked in New Look when I was younger, but I've never wanted to open a fashion store. There was another story after the World Cup about how a TV company was making a reality show with some of the girls, giving each of us our own boutique for a week and seeing which one of us could make the most money. If I was going to be in it then nobody told me! I think the whole shop thing came about because Dawn's company was building our house at the time and she told me that two years earlier she'd thought about buying that same shop. The bit about me was totally made up.

'Coleen Turns New Mansion into Chav Paradise'

When we bought our new house in Cheshire there were loads of rumours about what we were going to have in it, the interior design, the decorations. It was just cheap and petty gossip that was really snobbish. They made everything sound really terrible, as though we had no taste. It was that Chav rubbish again. The list was endless. I was meant to be having a swimming pool built with pink tiles. I was going to install my very own spray-tanning booth – for the record I don't do fake tans. I was going to have my own hairdresser's in there, and a seven-metre-length breakfast bar … How big did they think the kitchen was going to be?! The list went on. Then they said I was going to spend £50,000 on Christmas lights and that it was going to be like a mini Blackpool, and I was inviting the whole family round for the big switch-on. We had three Christmas trees that year, two small ones and a big one outside the house. So it was all rubbish. I think if people came round to our home they'd be surprised, because it's the opposite of how the newspapers have portrayed it to be.

'Heavies Guard Coleen after Hate Mail Blitz'

This one was almost true. The story claimed that I'd hired two ex-SAS men as security after receiving hate mail from a jealous female. There weren't any SAS soldiers involved but there was a period when hate mail about me started arriving, not to me but to my mum and other people. To this day we don't know who it was, but by their nature we guessed they were from a woman, just by the things they said. One referred to my Channel Five documentary *Being Coleen*, and said they'd seen me walking into Croxteth Sports Centre and how I had big tree-trunk legs and my bum was wobbling. I watched the documentary again and I thought, 'Oh shame, look at the size of my bum! It did look massive in those jeans and it was wiggling!' Only girls pick on those kinds of things. That sounds funny, but it was very scary and real at the time. All the letters were the same, horrible bits about me either cut up or photocopied from the newspaper, and next to them was written a nasty insult about my life, or how my friends were 'a bunch of scallies'. Posted from different boxes all over Liverpool, the letters were addressed to my mum, but she didn't tell me about them for a while. Some went to my dad, and they even sent them to the sunbed shop where my friend worked, saying about me, 'Your friend is embarrassing.' Eventually, we got the police involved and even hired a private investigator to try to catch this person. Then the story broke in the newspapers and we received one more letter saying, 'This is the last letter I'm going to send.' After that the letters stopped but we never discovered who'd been sending them. It had been a frightening and horrible situation to have to deal with.

'Mills and Roon – Coleen Pens Love Story'

This was plain silly and just goes to show how the tabloids will print anything to fill space. According to the *Daily Star* in 2006 I was halfway through writing a Jackie Collins-style novel – but without the sex. It was, they said, a tale about a girl's dreams of becoming a Hollywood star, but apparently I was too embarrassed to pen the raunchy bits! Another one of my so-called, unnamed 'pals' was quoted as saying, 'Coleen dreams of becoming the new Jackie Collins and writing a best-seller, but she's not one for writing the steamy bits.' Unbelievably, they even made up a quote from me. 'I'm not writing sex scenes. It's just not me,' I was supposed to have said! That was fiction about fiction. I've never read a Jackie Collins novel in my life.

'Coleen Approached to Go On *I'm a Celebrity* ...'

I think lots of people are approached to go on those kinds of programmes, and although I can't quite remember I was probably asked via my agent to go in the jungle for *I'm a Celebrity ... Get Me Out of Here*. However, the only reality show I think I would ever consider appearing on would be *Strictly Come Dancing*. It's one of my favourite programmes because it's just not like all those others. It's not really reality TV, it's just good entertainment. I'd never fancy doing *Big Brother*, and as for *I'm a Celebrity ...*, as much as I love it, I don't think I would be able to last in the jungle for more than five minutes, but you never know, I may feel differently about it in years to come. Also, with those kinds of programmes you put your career on the line. You either come out looking better or the opposite happens. If your career is going okay then I don't see any point in putting yourself through that kind of ordeal.

chapter eleven

photo-shoots and the art of breathing in

You never get used to walking into your local supermarket or newsagent and seeing your face on the cover of a magazine. I still get excited, especially if I like the photograph, and, fortunately, most of the time I do. One of the best parts of my working life right now is being invited by editors to appear in fashion shoots for their magazines. Over the past few years I've been in quite a few, from *Closer* to *Vogue*, and from *You* to *Marie Claire*. Then, on top of that, there's my advertising work for the likes of Asda, where I am the face of the George clothing 'must-have' range, and LG mobile phones. I have also done work for the National Lottery and, more recently, I had the opportunity to work with Wayne on a Christmas-themed electronic billboard poster in Piccadilly Square for Coca-Cola – Wayne representing Coke Zero and me representing Diet Coke.

The idea of doing a fashion shoot does sound glamorous, doesn't it? And, don't get me wrong, it is. But it's also an eight-hour job, sometimes longer, occasionally involving early-morning calls at 5 a.m. to catch the right sunlight, or late finishes in a studio or an empty house somewhere in South London, when you've had to do umpteen outfit swaps in a cramped toilet because there's nowhere else to change, and the photographer is asking if he can fit 'just one more shot' in. It's not so glamorous then.

All fashion shoots are different, depending on whether you're working for a magazine like *Closer*, who deal more in high street labels, or the glossies like *Vogue* and *Marie Claire*, who have the pick of the designers, but shoots can also be pretty similar in how they run. And at every shoot you go on you learn something different, and get better at doing your job and giving the photographer what they are looking for.

The first shoot I ever did was for the *Sunday Mirror* in 2004, and I didn't know what to expect. These days all requests will either go through our manager Paul or through my publicist Charlotte, but back then the *Sunday Mirror* phoned my mum's house directly. I asked Wayne about it, and he didn't mind, so not long afterwards my mum and I travelled down to London to the shoot location, which was at an old manor house. I look back now on that shoot and I just cringe. Everyone was nice, but the stylist put me in these long dresses and the way my hair and make-up were done just wasn't me. When the pictures came out I looked about fifty! At the time I didn't have the confidence to give them my opinions on what fashions and looks suited me best, and what I didn't appreciate then but do now is that the key to a good shoot is the relationship between you and the photographer. The more comfortable you feel, the better the shot that he or she gets. They were honestly the worst photographs I've ever done, probably not helped by the fact that I didn't know what I was doing. I didn't even know how to stand in front of the camera or the rules of breathing in when you are having your picture taken.

When I say breathing in, it's not really about hiding your belly. That would actually be quite hard for me anyway, because I know I've always had a bit of a tummy! Nothing major, but I know I've never had a flat stomach either. On the first few shoots I was involved in I was forever being told to breathe in. A girl could take that kind of thing personally but the reality is that it's more about posture than anything else. You get a better photograph if you are sitting properly or standing the correct way. Believe me, no one would ever insult you on a shoot – well, not to your face at least. I mean, it is fashion! Very soon you realize that everyone there, from the photographer down to the make-up artist, only ever wants you to look your best, because they want their work to be talked about as well.

All of this was new to me when I left our old house in Croxteth and caught the aeroplane down to London for that first shoot, but over time every experience teaches you new lessons and nowadays photo-shoots have become a normal and regular part of my working life.

Most shoots follow a similar pattern. In the first place, if it's a magazine like *Vogue* or *Marie Claire* or one of the newspaper supplements, a request will be put in to my publicist weeks, sometimes months, in advance. Depending on who it is and what they want to do, I'll either say yes or no. If it's a yes then the magazine will give an outline of their idea – or 'concept', as they often say. I should tell you at this point, because people often ask, that most magazines don't pay you to be in their pages. The newspapers will offer money and magazines like *OK!*, *Hello!*, *Heat* and *Closer* do, but fashion magazines don't. So why do I do it? Well, in terms of the glossies like *Vogue*, it's a magazine I've always loved and read, and the idea of being in it is great. On a purely business level, as Charlotte who works for my publicists, Ian Monk Associates, would tell you, it's also good for my profile. At other times I might agree because I have something to promote, like my George campaign for Asda, or my fitness DVD, or even this book. That's the way all magazines and newspapers work.

So if we say yes to a shoot either the fashion editor or the feature editor will speak to Charlotte about what they have in mind, just in case they're planning on a Page 3 concept or something, so there are not too many surprises when I turn up on the day! At this stage they will also ask for dress and shoe sizes. Occasionally, I might talk to them directly about what look they are going for and the kind of designer labels I like. That's what happened with the *Vogue* shoot. Their fashion editor, Kate Phelan, called and we spoke about which fashion designers I preferred. There have been one or two additions to the list over the last couple of years, but generally my favourites have stayed the same – Stella McCartney, Lanvin, Chloé and Missoni. I love Prada, especially for their bags and shoes, and a little bit of Gucci, but a lot of Prada's clothes tend to be a bit more formal and tailored, more grown-up. Those would be my choices, but then again, it depends on the fashions and the collections of the moment. For instance, if I'd been asked a few years ago then I would never have said Balenciaga, but now I love it. My taste is more feminine and girly-girl, along the lines of Chloé.

Photo-shoots and the art of breathing in   **171**

Inspire me!

You can find inspiration for fashion almost everywhere. Here are a few of my favourite places to find some fresh ideas:

1. **Party pages.** A magazine's fashion pages might give you a sense of style direction, but to find out what really works and what doesn't work, keep an eye out on their party pages for who's wearing what and what's wearing who these days.

2. **Take a trip back in time.** Pick up your remote, flick through the channels on satellite telly and find the classic movie channel TCM, or VH1 Classic for musical inspiration. Whether it's Julie Christie in *Doctor Zhivago* or an Eighties video of The Bangles singing 'Eternal Flame' (long before Atomic Kitten's version) you're bound to discover some new ideas.

3. **Vintage magazines.** Trends go round and round, so be the first by picking up old copies of *Vogue*, or even classic long-gone titles like *Nova* and *Honey*.

4. **Timeless beauties.** You can never go far wrong by studying the style and elegance of Hollywood greats like Audrey Hepburn, Sophia Loren and Grace Kelly.

5. **Play that funky music.** From rock to R&B, Kasabian to Kelis, what starts in the charts ends up on the catwalk.

6. **Cinema world.** Today's films influence tomorrow's fashions, whether that be *The Devil Wears Prada* Manhattan chic or the regal loveliness of *Marie Antoinette*.

It's horrible, but I know that some designers complain about the girls wearing their clothes, as if it somehow cheapens them, or at least that's what the newspapers report. Maybe it's true. (The bit about the designers, not the footballers' wives and girlfriends cheapening their clothes, that is!) To be honest, I don't listen to that kind of criticism. I'm sure if we didn't buy the clothes then they'd moan as well. Sometimes you can't win.

For a photo-shoot the fashion editor will also suggest a few labels, and unless I'm really anti a designer, I won't complain. After all, it's always great to try on new clothes!

In the days leading up to the shoot, someone from the magazine might call Charlotte and ask if I have any dietary requirements or preferences. This is the bit where some celebrities get a bad name for themselves. My response is always the same: 'Anything!' I don't mind what they get in for breakfast or lunch. I used to think everyone was the same as me, but apparently some people put in all kinds of strange demands, telling the magazine they are on some diet or other and won't eat this or that. I've been on loads of photoshoots and everyone has said I'm dead easy to work with, which is a compliment, but it also makes you wonder what they usually have to deal with, because I just think I'm being normal.

Finally, there's what's known as the 'call sheet'. This will arrive a couple of days before the shoot itself, and basically it's a 'who, what, where and when' schedule, giving the names of everyone on the shoot, the location address, other contact details, when it's going to finish, etc.

Strike a pose

When I first started shooting for magazines I had no idea what I was meant to do. Since then I've worked with some great photographers and picked up a few tricks of the trade, which, whether I'm shooting for *Vogue* or posing with my mates, should guarantee a better picture:

Practice makes perfect

It sounds a bit vain, I know, but stand in front of the mirror and figure out what expressions and angles suit you best. Go for it, no one's watching!

Don't stand straight on to the camera

Turn at the waist a little. Everyone's got a best side.

Take a deep breath and stand tall

The better your posture, the better the shot.

Light fantastic

Good lighting can make a photograph. The best time to take a picture outside is in the early morning when the sun's high, or in the late afternoon.

No over-the-top pouting!

Under any circumstances.

Say cheese!

Everyone looks good when they're smiling.

I'll travel down to London for the shoot itself. The shoots are nearly always in London because that's where the magazines are based, and where most of the good studios are. Usually, it's a half-nine or ten o'clock start, so that means waking up at about 6 a.m. and travelling down from Manchester or Liverpool by train. I've got to confess that I'm not very good at getting up in the mornings. Once I'm up and about I'm all right, kind of, but I hate early mornings. If you are travelling down on the train with me at seven o'clock in the morning then don't expect me to speak to you! Then again, if you're with me on the way back I'll chew your ear off!

The journey down from home to London only lasts a couple of hours or so, so that's not too bad, and I tend to do the return journey on the same day. I'm always offered the opportunity of staying over in a hotel, but unless Wayne's playing away in Europe with Man United or England then I prefer to travel back home.

The general rule seems to be that the bigger the magazine, the more people there are on the shoot. As well as the photographer, fashion editor, hairdresser and make-up artist, everyone has their own assistant, sometimes two or three in the case of the photographers. Then there might be someone else from the magazine, like the Creative Director or the Photography Director, and sometimes they have assistants too! Occasionally there will be a manicurist and then, depending on the budget, there will be outside caterers to prepare the food and look after everyone. So quite a few people in total, then.

In the beginning it was quite daunting walking into that kind of crowd, but over time I've got used to being in a room full of strange faces. I'll say 'Hi!', be introduced to everyone and just make general chit-chat. People are usually really pleasant and laid back.

To be honest, I'm often so knackered from the journey I can barely string a sentence together! Breakfast will be laid on and maybe I'll have a slice of toast.

The shoot is quite easy-going, or at least it is from my perspective. If I've turned up at ten o'clock then everyone else has probably been there for at least an hour to set things up beforehand. After breakfast, the fashion editor will ask if I want to come and see the clothes and maybe try a few things on before having my hair and make-up done. It varies, because on some shoots there will be a few outfits, then at others, like *Vogue* and *Marie Claire*, there will be a whole rail of clothes, and throughout the day motorcycle couriers will arrive with more outfits and accessories. Imagine your dream dressing-up day when you were a little girl, and it's a bit like that.

If something doesn't suit me then I'll try on something else. The fashion editor will have ideas and hopefully I'll agree with them. I've got more confident these days in saying what I do and don't like, so I'm not afraid of telling them if I dislike something. At first I used to be a bit embarrassed about changing in front of strangers, but now I just don't think twice about it, it doesn't bother me because I'm there for a job.

I'll try on the outfits they've put together and talk about how I feel about them, whether I like them, whether I feel comfortable in them, etc. Occasionally, if the clothes don't fit, the fashion editor's assistant might have to pin the back with safety pins or bulldog clips That's something you don't see in the photographs when they appear in the magazine! After about an hour or so we'll make the final choice and I'll move on to hair and make up, leaving the fashion team to steam the clothes, or perhaps make some on-the-spot alterations.

The next step is a chat with the hair stylist and the make-up artist. The hair stylist will most probably pin my hair back or put it in curlers before I sit in the make-up chair.

As far as make-up goes, if it's going to be a shoot that reflects me I prefer to go for a more natural look, but, for instance, they might say they're going to do a bit more with my eyes, and I'll go along with it. Once it's done we can make a decision and say whether we're going to tone it down or not. You've got to learn to appreciate the difference between seeing your make-up done in the mirror and how your face will look in a photograph. There is always going to be a little exaggeration with your make-up, but once you see yourself in the Polaroid, or on the computer screen if the photographer's working in digital, it's only then that you truly understand what the make-up artist has been aiming for.

Once the make-up is over I'll go to sit with the hairstylist and their assistant. I've had my hair done in so many ways, but usually they'll simply put a few curlers in. I've got hair extensions, but that doesn't really affect the styling and they just treat it as they would normal hair. I'm quite open to ideas, though.

Hair and make-up are always working with the fashion editor to create an overall look. So, for example, I've done a kind of rock 'n' roll bobby-sox girl shoot for *You* magazine and gone 'vamp' for *Closer* – it all depends on what's in fashion at the time.

Over the course of a day, I might do three or four different 'looks', which can involve a few sessions in the make-up chair and with the hairstylist. Other people might get irritated at all those changes but I actually love having my hair and make-up done. I like people playing with my hair. I find it soothing and relaxing.

Before we start the actual shoot itself I'll have a conversation with the photographer and they'll talk me through what direction they want to go in. More often than not it's a man, and he will just try to put me at ease and explain how they want me to be in front of the camera.

In reality, it's not that easy to stand there and pose for someone I've just met with a fashion team looking on. It's totally different from the pictures I take with family and friends. Throughout my life, growing up, all I can remember of family occasions is me standing there and smiling for photos. That comes naturally. But for the first photo-shoots I was in I felt a bit weird and self-conscious, so I didn't know what to do. My big fear was that they'd plonk me in front of the camera and I'd be stood there having to work out for myself what positions the photographer wanted me in, while they stood there snapping away.

It's not like that. A good photographer will guide me as the shoot progresses, telling me what pose to take up, and if I'm not doing it right then they will suggest something different. Every photographer wants to capture the best picture, and so they always want to get the best out of me. As time's gone on, I've picked up advice from all the photographers I've worked with, so I'm more confident in what I'm doing now. I know when to change my head position, or to alter the expression on my face, or to turn so my hair moves differently. But, still, the photographer instructs me as we go along. They'll talk me through everything, and hopefully I give them what they want.

If the photographer is working on a digital camera they'll have a computer screen set up. Pretty often they'll notice something I don't see, good or bad, and I either have to correct myself for the next shot or trust that the photographer has got the image they are looking for. Working with a photographer is all about trust, which is why the A listers and the supermodels have their favourites.

The one time I really get to talk to everyone is when we break for lunch. It's great for everyone else, but sometimes, if I'm wearing a tight-fitting dress, then I do think twice about eating that piece of bread because I know it's going to bloat me out. But most of the time I eat the same as everyone else. The crew on *Closer* are always dialling out for Japanese sushi, or even Italian. The food on shoots is usually really healthy – salads, fish, cold meat, that kind of thing – and I'll eat to suit the way I'm feeling on the day. If I'm hungry I won't starve myself, but if I'm on a diet then I'll watch what goes in my stomach. Shoots can cost thousands of pounds, so I have a responsibility to fulfil my part of the deal and be professional, and that means looking good for the camera. I don't get upset when someone asks me to 'Breathe in!' or 'Stand taller!', or they mess around with me like I'm a doll. I would never consider myself as a model, but on the days when I'm shooting then you've got to appreciate that that's what you are.

An entire shoot will usually last up to eight hours, and believe me it does feel like a whole working day. I feel tired at the end of it. People think I turn up and simply stand in front of the camera, which I do to a certain extent, but the entire process of swapping outfits, being in and out of the make-up chair, the hairstylist's chair, being pinned up, and simply waiting around while the next shot is prepared, can take it out of me. Such days can be really fun and enjoyable, but I don't know if I would describe them as glamorous. The glamorous part is seeing the results.

After I've left the location or the studio my part of the job is done. The next time I'll see the photographs will be when the magazine comes out on the shelves. In between, the photographer will have worked on the shots at his studio, retouching or airbrushing out any blemishes, etc. I know there has been a lot of discussion in the newspapers about the way photographs are retouched, and how celebrities look nothing like their photos in the pages of a magazine. It happens. The photographer will take out a crease in a dress, or remove some other mark that's not been noticed on the shoot. I don't get told about these things, but I think I might notice if there'd been some major work done, like stretching me to make my legs seem longer! I wouldn't really like that, because it wouldn't be me, and I wouldn't want to come across as anyone other than myself in photographs.

Shooting for magazines has become an essential part of my career, defining me as Coleen, an individual in my own right, rather than simply the girlfriend of Wayne Rooney the footballer. And Wayne's been really supportive in encouraging me to pursue this path. He's often away playing football with either his club or England, and rather than me being stuck at home he's keen to see me succeed in this kind of media work.

And I'm happy too. I went shopping with my mum and we popped into Asda. We walked in, looked to our left, and there I was in my Asda campaign. It's a strange feeling when I see something like that, or when I go to the magazines and there I am on the front cover of one I wasn't expecting. Quite often magazines will buy in an old shoot I've done for someone else and use it on their front cover. Shoppers must look at me flicking through *More* or *Woman's Own* in the supermarket, thinking, 'Doesn't she get the magazine sent to her? Look at her, flicking through the magazines ogling pictures of herself!' I don't mind what other people think, I'm still as excited at seeing myself in a magazine as the first time I had my photograph taken.

chapter twelve

we're not all called chardonnay or cristal

Tell someone you go out with a Premiership footballer, or you are engaged to one, or even if the two of you are married, and there are a lot of people who immediately draw their own conclusions about the type of girl you are. It's all about the money, they say. It's about designer labels and designer jewellery, flash cars and champagne. It's about fame. Their stereotype of the footballer's wife or girlfriend seems to be all about bad taste, greed, Sunday newspaper kiss 'n' tell stories and controversy, as if our day-to-day lives are some kind of over-the-top soap opera. For both positive and negative reasons, I think people like to believe that we are a real-life version of the television programme *Footballers' Wives*, and the newspapers and weekly magazines reinforce that view. They love to play up the soap-opera aspects of our lives, and, well, if there isn't a story this week then they'll make one up. But the reality of being engaged to Wayne, being married to or going out with a footballer, isn't quite as it's portrayed in the television series. I'm not saying that it can't be glamorous, or that there isn't a clubbing scene out there full of girls wanting to bag a footballer, or that, like in any walk of life, there isn't a seedy side to it all. However, speaking for myself, I don't recognize that TV version of our lives. It doesn't really tell you what it's like to be engaged to a Premiership footballer and a professional athlete.

Footballers' Wives **has a lot to answer for! Everything about it is totally blown out of all proportion, even down to how the girls get dressed up to the nines in designer labels to go to a match on a Saturday. No one does that. It's just not practical for starters.**

I used to go in my jeans, and if it's winter you make sure you're wearing a big coat, because it's freezing when you're sat outside for ninety minutes.

These days I have my own executive box, but even then I don't go over the top. The girls in *Footballers' Wives* dress up like they are going on a night on the town.

Not that me and Wayne didn't used to watch the show when it was on. Well, that was when we first met and we were sixteen years old. Actually, there's a funny story about that time. One night the two of us were going out, so we asked Wayne's mum if she could tape *Footballers' Wives* for us to watch when we came back. So we arrived home, stuck the video in and sat back and started watching the episode. The programme finished and the next thing we know we're staring at some porno video! I was just sitting there not knowing what to do. We were only sixteen and had just started seeing each other. Next thing, Wayne's calling his brother all sorts, and we ran into his brother's bedroom and started whacking him round the head with the tape. Wayne's brother had stitched us up. I'll never forget that.

But I'm going off the subject a little. There is a stereotype about the kinds of girls who go after footballers, and, to a certain degree, as far as the club scene goes it's not far from the truth. Every now and again I'll go to a club in Liverpool, and as soon as we walk in there's a couch full of girls just sitting there waiting to see if there's anyone worth pulling. They're dressed in all this skimpy gear, exactly how you imagine the glamour girls to look. I know that some of them already have a reputation for going with players, and you'll see that as soon as one walks into the club they're up at the bar all over him. It's not a very nice atmosphere really.

The girls are unbelievable sometimes, but then again, there are some footballers who love all the attention.

I've had conversations with some of the other girls about that scene, and we all have our different tales to tell. How we'll go into a club, and girls will be coming on to our boyfriends, as if we don't exist. They'll come up and say 'Hiya!' and all that, introduce themselves to the players, and treat us like we're invisible, even though we're stood there next to him. I remember a friend saying how when she was pregnant she went out to a nightclub with all the players, wives and girlfriends after the team's Christmas party. She was in this club and it's full of lovely, lovely girls and, well, she was pregnant, so she didn't feel as good about her body as she'd usually feel. But because she wasn't drinking she was really alert to everything that was going on and she couldn't believe the way the girls were just all over the players, even though many were with their partners.

I once heard this story about a player and his girlfriend who were going to a nightclub. Their car pulls up at the door, the two of them get out and there are all these photographers screaming his name and all these girls throwing themselves at him. The player was so desperate to get inside that he left his girlfriend behind outside!

It does make you think differently about other girls. I mean, there's no such thing as a sisterhood in that scene. It happened to me and Wayne. Not that long ago, we were in a bar with friends and the two of us were just talking, when this woman came up to Wayne and started saying something. Wayne gets people coming up to him all the time saying stupid things and we just learn to ignore them. So we tried that, and Wayne was giving her a look as if to tell her to go away. Next thing, she's waving this tenner at him. It's funny, but for some reason people sometimes ask him to sign money. So she's stood there waving this tenner and she won't go away. Next thing, she's asking him to go and buy her a drink because they've called last orders at the bar and they won't serve her. I just thought, 'How cheeky are you?!'

The girls are unbelievable sometimes, but then again, there are some footballers who love all the attention. The girls throw themselves at these lads, and at the end of the day they're an easy catch. It's no surprise that there are footballers out there who will go for all that and take advantage of what's on offer, because they know there's a queue of girls lining up. So it's hard to say who's taking advantage of who. I'm sure there are some girls out there who are simply attracted to footballers, but then there are others who want them for the wrong reasons, and they are likely to turn up in the Sunday papers the following weekend telling all.

We're not all called Chardonnay or Cristal   **189**

I think that incident in a Manchester bar called Panacea involving me, Wayne and the Blackburn Rovers footballer Michael Gray illustrates the way some players feel about the girls in these clubs.

Most of our footballer friends, who Wayne's known from his Everton days or has become close friends with at Manchester United, are all in long-term relationships, so I've never really seen any new girls come onto the scene.

I can understand why you find a lot of celebrities going out together and falling in love. They probably mix in the same circles, and feel safe in each other's company because they are in the same boat.

Touch wood, but I think that if me and Wayne ever did split up, it would be very hard for him to find someone he could really trust, a girl who didn't just want to go out with him because he's Wayne Rooney, the famous footballer. It is difficult. If you're in a

relationship in his business then you've got to trust the person you're with, and that can be hard to find. I've grown up with Wayne and Wayne's grown up with me. I've learned from him and vice versa. Trust in any relationship is important, but it's especially so when you're in the spotlight.

If you are really in love with someone you shouldn't have to feel suspicious or question their motives, but unfortunately footballers attract the kinds of girls who are out there either for the fame or to make a few grand from the newspapers.

Of course, not all girls are the same and there are loads of relationships, whether it's with footballers or otherwise, that start in nightclubs and everyone lives happily ever after. What is annoying is that all footballers' wives and girlfriends are tarred with the same brush. One of Wayne's friends is the Everton player Alan Stubbs, and a while back we went to his bar launch in Liverpool. I was talking to Alan's wife, Mandy, and that day she'd read something negative about me and the footballers' wives in the newspaper. She was fuming, saying, 'Well, I'm a footballer's wife and I'm not like that!' And that's how a lot of the girls feel. They have families and children, and being a footballer's wife as shown in the TV programme isn't anywhere near what it's truly like.

The newspapers are only too ready to make a girl famous just because she's going out with a footballer – they will give her money for a story and a photo-shoot. Now before everyone says it, isn't that what happened to me? But it's not. I know I have done a few photo-shoots for newspapers. But I never went out of my way to capture fame. It was the other way round – fame grabbed me and I have had to deal with it as positively as I can. It's no wonder certain girls find the prospect of that kind of fame and reward attractive. But, at the same time, that newspaper will turn around the next week and slag her off, asking what does that girl do other than go out with a famous footballer. The newspapers want it all ways. The interest in the wives and partners of footballers is a relatively new phenomenon, which in many ways has been manufactured by the media to fill all the newspapers and celebrity titles that are on the news stands these days. That's fair enough, but it doesn't mean we're all the same. We didn't all walk into a nightclub one Saturday night and stagger out with a footballer on our arm.

I've heard that Wayne's manager, Sir Alex Ferguson, likes his players to be settled down and in a steady relationship. That's just being realistic, because if a lad's a bit wild and enjoys his social life a bit too much then he's not going to perform on a Saturday. There's no way a top-class footballer can be at his peak if he's out on the town every other night. I might go out with my mates, but Wayne really doesn't go out that often. He has matches once, sometimes twice, a week and the rest of the time he's training. Every now and again we go to a club or a bar in Manchester or Liverpool, but he much prefers going out for a quiet meal or going round to friends for dinner.

What people on the outside often don't appreciate is that when you're in a relationship with a footballer then your life is dictated by the fixture list and their training schedule.

At a club like Manchester United you can be playing Premiership matches one week and then Champions' League the next, then in between there will be England matches and cup competitions. Being a professional footballer is all about commitment and dedication and sacrifice, and if you're the partner then it means you're left on your own a lot of the time while they're away. Sometimes, with England, Wayne will be away for ten days at a time, so while he's gone I'll see loads of my mum and dad. I do get lonely if I'm left on my own but, being positive, I think it's good for our relationship to spend time apart, otherwise we'd probably get under each other's feet all the time and on each other's nerves!

If it's a normal week, Wayne leaves the house at 8.30 a.m. to head off for the Manchester United training ground near our house in Cheshire. He'll arrive back home at about 2.30 p.m., but he may well have other club or sponsorship commitments to deal with after that.

When Manchester United have a home match at Old Trafford then, normally, he'll stay the night at a hotel and the next time I'll see him is after the match. Usually, if it's a midweek evening kick-off then he's allowed to stay at home.

You would think that having to go out and perform at the top of your game in front of seventy-odd thousand supporters might make you a little bit nervous, but Wayne's very laid back, and seeing him at home before a match you'd never imagine he had a big game ahead. The only time I see him frustrated is when he's been banned from playing and he has to sit out a few games. All he ever wants to do is be out on the pitch.

On the day of a game, I'll go down with family and friends an hour before kick-off and we'll have a meal in our executive box. I moved to a box from a seat in the stands as my work started to develop. Many times I would be sat trying to watch the game when people would want my autograph or a picture, which was no problem but it meant I wasn't able to enjoy the day with my family as much. I still do love watching games from the stands and, on most occasions when Wayne plays for England, that's what I do, normally with my dad and brothers. I love the atmosphere, the songs and the cheering, and my dad loves it when the Mexican wave gets going.

Once the match is over, we'll wait for Wayne to finish showering and changing, then go home. There isn't really much in the way of socializing with the other players and their partners. People might think there's a really glitzy players' lounge at Old Trafford where everyone hangs out after a game, but it's only a tiny room with a small bar, and it's usually full of guests of the club, prize-winners, that kind of thing.

I've met Wayne's boss, Sir Alex Ferguson, a couple of times. Once was when Wayne first signed for Man United. Occasionally, the club organizes get-togethers, such as when we were invited out to Portugal for part of the pre-season build-up, or they might have a party after something like the FA Cup Final. We had that in 2005 in Cardiff. It would have been better had Manchester United won, but they ended up losing on penalties to Arsenal. That was horrible, actually. Alongside the two matches against Portugal in the Euros and the World Cup, it must rank as the most upset and down I've seen Wayne after a match.

Wayne hates losing but usually he's not narky or anything when he gets home. He'll just go quiet and won't feel like doing much. If the team has lost and he feels he hasn't played to his full potential then that's worse and he'll have a big cob on. But if he feels he's played well personally then he'll just go out and get on with it.

Usually Wayne will come home from a game and he's so pumped up with adrenaline that, especially when it's a night match, he finds it hard to sleep. I love my sleep. Once the soaps are over, I'm looking to go to bed at ten, ten thirty, but Wayne won't be able to sleep, so he'll stay up watching a film or even the match all over again until around one o'clock in the morning.

I think the biggest misconception about footballers' wives and girlfriends is that we all hang out together.

From Manchester United, me and Wayne are really good mates with Rio Ferdinand, John O'Shea, Wes Brown and their partners Rebecca, Yvonne and Leanne. As far as the England team goes, the reality is that you only see the girls when there's a tournament or a get-together. It's not like we're all on the phone to each other every week saying let's all go for a night out.

Even when we're away together, I think the public would be surprised how far the newspapers' version of people and events differs from what everyone's actually like and what really goes on.

Over in Baden-Baden during the 2006 World Cup it was portrayed as if we were partying every night. It wasn't like that at all. There was one restaurant called Garibaldi's which at night turned into a bit – and I mean a bit – of a bar. My auntie and uncle came over to Germany for a few days and she was saying, 'Is this the place where you're supposed to be dancing every night? It looked like a nightclub in the newspapers.' They were really disappointed!

Oi! Referee! Blow your whistle!

The thing about stereotypes is that so often they're true. If you are looking to emulate the style of the footie wives and girlfriends then be sure to avoid the following:

Obvious designer overload

Stepping out wearing the same designer's print from head to toe isn't a fashion statement, it's a sponsorship deal.

Flashing the flesh

A little bare flesh and you're going for elegance, too much and you're going to get a reputation!

Faking it

Boobs, lips, teeth, tans. Try to keep it real – well, at least one of them.

Obvious logos

Who wants to look like a human advertising hoarding?

White stilettos with a high tackiness rating

It's true what they say ...

Absolutely ghetto fabulous

Don't overdo the bling. Discretion is the key, so limit yourself with the dazzling jewellery.

Where we were staying, Brenner's Park Hotel, was dead quiet. We'd go out for a drink on a night but not that many. The trouble was that all the newspapers sent a team of reporters over and it was their job to find a story or make one up out of nothing.

One night there were two journalists who trailed us everywhere. They were in Garibaldi's all the time, drinking more than us. Towards the end of the tournament I got really tired of being followed all the time. I turned around to one of them and said, 'Haven't you got a wife at home?' He said he had, so I asked him what she thought of him following young girls around all day long. He didn't put that in the newspaper. Instead he asked me what designer my dress was and I told him Chloé. Then I said, 'Who's your suit by?' He said, 'Hugo Boss.' So I just had a go at him for going on about our designer clothes when there he was in his Hugo Boss suit. That conversation just highlighted the stupidity of it all.

The girls couldn't win during that tournament. Had we not been out there then the newspapers would have gone on about Coleen going shopping in Manchester when she should have been supporting Wayne in Germany. You can never do the right thing.

GMTV, amongst others, had a reporter standing outside our hotel virtually every morning, asking us, 'What do you think of Baden-Baden?' I was thinking, 'You're here the same way we are, can't you tell people what Baden-Baden's like?' It was just silly. There were reports that the local fashion boutiques like Gucci had ordered in an extra £200,000 worth of clothes to make sure they didn't sell out, or how I was meant to have spent £900 in ten minutes on three pairs of Gucci shoes, or how we had a £400 drinks bill at the end of one evening – which isn't that much if there's a lot of you and you're out for a night.

All these stories build up the myth of footballers' wives and girlfriends, and I suppose to someone on the outside they're entertaining enough, but they don't paint the whole picture and often they are way off the mark.

If the journalists told it how it really was then nobody would buy their newspaper. If they told you that Victoria Beckham is actually a really good laugh with a great sense of humour then no one would be interested. She is, but people are more interested in hearing made-up stories about the girls being at war and how Victoria keeps herself to herself. Those are the stories people want to read, not the boring truth.

The pictures in the newspapers tell you nothing. Until you actually speak to someone you'll never know what they're about. It's the same being the partner of a footballer. Unless you've been there you can't know what the life is truly like.

chapter thirteen

don't stop shopping 'til you've had enough…

So maybe I've got this reputation for being a shopaholic. Okay, not maybe, I have got this reputation for being a shopaholic. But it's not true. Yes, I like shopping, but I'm not addicted to abusing the plastic on a daily basis. I don't need help, thank you very much!

The shopaholic tag dates back to the very beginning when I began going out with Wayne and the newspapers started taking pictures of me. He was with Everton at the time, while I'd left school, and the only occasions anyone ever saw me was around Croxteth or in Liverpool city centre with a bundle of shopping bags in my hands. The newspapers were interested in who Wayne's girlfriend was but because there were no skeletons in my cupboard they had nothing to print. So, instead, they invented this shopping persona. I might have only been going out shopping once or twice a week, but because I wasn't doing anything else they were the only pictures they could take. It got to the stage when photographs of me coming out of supermarkets with a load of groceries were making newspapers. Or I'd come out of my mum's with a plastic bag and they'd be snapping away. It was idiotic. The photographers and reporters would give their business cards out to security men and shop assistants asking if they'd tip them off if they saw me out shopping.

At first I laughed it off, but then it did begin to annoy me. What wound me up more than anything was how they made out that all I was doing all day was going out spending Wayne's money. If you repeat those kinds of stories enough then it does affect the way people think about you. If for some reason my credit card doesn't go through, I've had shop assistants look at me and say, 'Have you been spending all that money again?' No, I haven't! Or I will have been down to London for a photo-shoot and someone will come up to me on the train on the way back asking if I've been on a shopping trip. I think, 'Oh, shut up!', because it's been going on for ages and ages now.

I don't think it's a question of me liking shopping, it's more to do with my love of fashion and clothes, as the two go hand in hand. As far as I'm concerned, they're one and the same. When I was at school, every now and again we'd have to fill out a question-naire and it would ask us what our hobbies were. I'd always write down 'shopping' as one of them, and, thinking back now, so did most of the girls in my class.

When I was a kid, thirteen or fourteen years old, going into Liverpool city centre on a Saturday and spending the whole afternoon with my mates shopping always used to be a big thing. About ten of us would meet up around dinner time, grab a drink from the shop and catch the Number 5 or the Number 14 bus from The Strand, the row of shops next to my mum and dad's house. We'd pay the lowest fare we could because we wanted to save all our money for when we were in town, then we'd all run upstairs to sit on the top deck, right at the back of the bus.

My mum and dad would give me pocket money every week. It used to be different amounts and sometimes as much as a tenner, but it never really lasted long in my pocket, so when it came to shopping I never really had any money. None of us really had any money, but that didn't stop us going round all the shops and looking. Topshop was always a favourite, then H&M. We wouldn't try the clothes on, we just used to say, 'I like that, I like this, I might get that for Easter.' Then we'd stop off at McDonald's for a burger. All the girls from our school used to be there, everyone in their little groups doing the same thing as us. After that, we'd head off to all the shoe shops like Ravel and Dolcis, trying on all the latest designs. We'd finish the day off by going to this shop called Quarters that sold hair bobbles and dress jewellery. I went through a real phase of buying hair bobbles all the time, and even though I didn't have much money I always made sure I had enough left to buy a few for a couple of pounds. I think they were only fifty pence each. Or I'd buy a lip-gloss or something. I really used to enjoy those Saturday shopping days with my mates. You go into Liverpool now and see girls the age I used to be doing exactly the same thing.

Nowadays I prefer shopping on my own. I like going with a mate or my mum or my Auntie, but I just feel like I'm dragging them round. If I'm going to the Trafford Centre in Manchester or Harvey Nichols then I like to make it more of a solo expedition. The only downside of that is if I get a photographer following me, because I feel stupid walking around with someone snapping away at me with their camera. As I said before, that's why sometimes, if I'm only nipping into town to go to one shop, I'll park on a double-yellow line so I can just run in and out and dodge the paparazzi. I know, it's bad. Usually, though, it's okay, I don't get pestered and I'm able to walk around the shops and try on clothes like any other girl.

I don't think it's a question of me liking shopping, it's more to do with my love of fashion and clothes, as the two go hand in hand.

If I'm shopping in Liverpool, I'll take a look around all the usual places – both high-street stores and the designer label shops. Fortunately my deal with Asda also means I get sent the latest Must Have designs before they arrive in store. In the past year they've done some great oversize knits and jersey tops.

There are a couple of boutiques I'll pop into as well called Peach and Drome. Then, of course, I'll go to see if there's anything new in Cricket on Matthew Street. When it first opened, Cricket used to be this tiny menswear shop, then Justine, the owner, started to sell womenswear. Nowadays, they've extended back and up, so you have menswear downstairs and women's fashion on the top floor. My Auntie Tracy and Uncle Shaun first introduced me to Cricket, but I must have been about sixteen years old when I began going there and buying little bits. In the beginning, I was really into my Juicy tracksuits. They were really big at the time and I bought my first one from there.

Because Liverpool hasn't got a Harvey Nichols or a Selfridges, Cricket has become the best place to go for all the top labels like Chloé, Stella McCartney and Marc Jacobs.

Justine's really good at predicting what's going to be popular so they always seem to be the first to get gear in. There will be waiting lists everywhere else, but, say with a Balenciaga bag or the Chloé Paddington bag with the big lock on, Justine will know there's going to be a demand and she'll make sure she's ordered enough for her customers. And, apart from the great

High-street high

You don't have to break the bank to look great. These are some of my favourite high-street must-have buys:

Basic cotton underwear from George at Asda
Cashmere jumpers from Gap
Silky satin blouses from Reiss
Black pants from Warehouse
Chunky cable-knit cardigans from George at Asda
Jackets from Zara
Simple plain vests and T-shirts from Topshop
Jeans from Topshop
And, of course, shift dresses from George at Asda

Coleen: welcome to my world

clothes, everyone who works there is really friendly. The girls don't have to wear uniform and they're all dead laid back. It's not like some designer shops you go to where the staff can sometimes look down on you.

I sound like an advert, don't I? Believe it or not, I'm not on any sort of commission or anything, and, just in case you wondered, I only get the usual 10 per cent discount for being a regular customer. It's just a great little shop and, over the years, Justine's helped me out with my fashion and become a good friend.

Sometimes I wonder if people think Cricket is this big Harvey Nichols-type store from the way it's written about in the magazines. I suppose I'm partly responsible, but these days loads of girls travel from all over the country to shop there, or even just to have a look around. Justine says there's one girl who comes in religiously every week, asking, 'Has Coleen been in today?' or 'Has Coleen bought anything lately?' It's really sweet. She won't buy anything, it's just that she likes to know what I'm wearing. Yeah, Cricket's become a Liverpool tourist attraction in its own right now. Tourists come to the city for The Beatles and Cricket! It's mad.

If I go down to London shopping, I'll usually stay at the Mandarin Hotel in Knightsbridge, which is a stone's throw away from Harvey Nichols. It's also near my favourite shopping street of all, Sloane Street, which has all the designer stores like Chloé, Prada and Yves Saint Laurent. If we're staying in a different hotel, me and Wayne might hire a driver to take us around all the different shops and wait outside. That sounds a bit indulgent, doesn't it? But, really, because there are so many more paparazzi down in London, it's just more practical. And it is nice to be driven round all day!

There are certain advantages to being recognized. For one thing, the assistants in the posher shops are probably a bit more helpful if they think you're going to spend lots of money, whereas if I'm abroad I still get those snooty looks from the staff. Last year in Cannes we moored the boat and I was wearing all my beach stuff, flip-flops, the usual. I also had my hair pulled back, and though I look young anyway, that made me appear even younger. I went into this designer store and I felt them staring in a funny way, as if to say, 'What does this little girl want?' I know it's a bit mean, but in those situations it's nice to get your credit card out and buy something really expensive. The assistants always react in the same way I react when I see someone buying a really expensive item – you wonder what they do for a living to afford that.

Like most girls, my weaknesses are bags and shoes. I couldn't tell you how many pairs of shoes I've got at home. Loads.

As far as favourite designers go, I'd say I was a big fan of Christian Louboutin, but then I also really like Marc Jacobs, Prada, Chloé … I could go on and on. I think I've got more shoes than bags, but the only reason is that bags tend to be a lot more expensive. If I had to give one up, then I'm afraid shoes would lose out every time. I love bags. I do admit to owning lots of handbags, but I really don't have a clue how many, I must count them one day and let you know! I keep them all in my dressing room at home, lined up on glass shelves. It's not that I just buy expensive bags, I'll buy a Topshop bag as well, but the

My Golden Rules of Shopping

It's a girl thing. Go shopping alone or with your mates. Boyfriends just get bored after one store.

If the shoe fits… When out shopping for a special outfit, i.e. for Christmas or a birthday, take the shoes you'll be wearing with you.

Think smalls. Buy underwear that can be worn with different looks. For example, with a camisole go for a bra with pretty straps, or with a hugging jersey dress wear a seamless bra.

Indecisions are final. If uncertain about a purchase, don't buy it if you prefer the outfit you're already wearing. That's your benchmark.

Shop for today. Don't buy clothes in the hope they'll one day be in. Buy for here and now.

Don't hang around. Get on the waiting list now. You can always change your mind nearer the time.

Best foot forward. Try shoes on early in the day. After lots of walking, feet tend to swell and you'll end up with the wrong size.

The early bird catches the bargains. Pick up the best of the new stock by shopping early in the season, i.e. January for spring, and July for winter.

Make friends. Pal up with the managers at your favourite stores. They'll get to know your style and will call you before new designs hit the shop floor.

Don't be a slave to fashion. Forget trends that don't suit you.

high-fashion designs are the ones I'll keep forever and use over and over again. That's the one thing about a good designer bag, I don't feel bad about being seen out with it on more than one day or night in the week. Whereas if I was seen wearing the same designer jumper for a week then I know people would think I was some kind of scruff!

When I was younger I was really into Juicy bags, but they're not so expensive. The first real designer bag I owned was a classic blue Balenciaga, which Wayne bought for me. Since then I've just kept collecting them. If you were to ask me to name the top ten bags I own then, at the moment, this would be it (although I'm sure this list might have one or two new entries by the time this book comes out):

1. Chloe Heloise
2. Fendi sweetbox clutch
3. Alexander McQueen Elvie
4. Stella McCartney large patent clutch
5. Lanvin shopper
6. Chanel padded classic
7. Yves Saint Laurent downtown
8. Balenciaga with large studs
9. Chanel large patent with gold chain handles
10. Prada two-toned patent

I've got to confess that part of the attraction of designer bags is owning a bag that no one else or very few people have, and beating the waiting list. There used to be a waiting list for the Fendi Spy bag so when Wayne went out to Japan with Manchester

United he picked one up for me there. It's exciting to know you're one of the first to own a particular design, when you're aware that there's a queue and that high-street shops will soon be bringing out their own version but you've got the original.

Invest in your fashion

Okay, so I'm lucky enough to be able to shop on quite a generous budget, but every girl needs to splash out now and again. Make the right choice and that big designer buy should last you a lifetime and save you money in the long run. That's what I say! These are some of my top fashion investments:

Classic leather bag. From Balenciaga, Hermès or Chloé.

Fitted black suit. By either Alexander McQueen or Stella McCartney.

Black high heels. They've got to be either Christian Louboutin, Manolo Blahnik or Prada.

Classic trench coat. What Burberry does best.

Jeans. Modern style from Sass & Bide and True Religion.

Diamond earrings. Chopard, Tiffany or Cartier only. A girl can wish, can't she!

I understand that some people wonder how I can justify spending all that money on one bag, but I do see it as a treat. And they do mean something to me. Often they mark an occasion or an event. The most I've ever spent is £2,000 on a Fendi bag, and I bought that as a keepsake after I'd just brought out my fitness DVD. I thought, 'I've worked for that bag. I've worked hard and that's my money I've earned and I can spend it on whatever I want.' I'm proud to use that bag.

One of the most annoying things about being labelled a shopaholic by the newspapers is the insinuation that I haven't got any money of my own and all I've ever done is spend Wayne's wages.

When we first started going out together, Wayne didn't even have a professional contract with Everton. He was on the YTS and he only earned about £60 a week. I think he bought me a pair of trainers once, but back then, in the early stages of our relationship, I would never take money from him. I was still living with my mum and dad and I got my own pocket money. Not only that but we weren't old enough to go into pubs or at an age when you ate out at posh restaurants so we didn't really need any money.

Further down the line, Wayne earned his first proper contract at Everton, and then he would buy me things or take me out shopping, or if I was going into town he'd give me some money to treat myself. He didn't give me money from the very start, as the newspapers made out. Even if he had done, it's really not anyone else's business, and I think a lot of criticism stems from pure jealousy.

Computer love

Whether you are shopping for online bargains or simply want to keep up with the latest catwalk trends and clothes gossip, log on to the Internet and get lost in fashion cyberspace. Check out:

www.net-a-porter.com

- from Chloé to Jimmy Choo, Fendi to Marc Jacobs, this is basically a luxury fashion magazine where you can buy everything you see straight away.

www.topshop.co.uk

- typically slick and simple, this will satisfy your Topshop fix 24/7.

www.style.com

- the online home of *Vogue* and *W* magazines, no fashion site competes with the next-day coverage and reviews of all the major catwalk shows, and a catwalk library that dates back to 2000. Their 'People and Parties' pages are definitely worth a regular nose too.

www.handbag.com

- great for celebrity fashion news and gossip.

www.asos.com

- this website used to be known as www.asSeenonScreen.com, but it still remains the best source for celeb fashion trends. Not only that, whatever the stars are wearing you can buy online.

When columnists write about my spending I just think they can't be happy with their own lives if they need to poke their noses into mine.

Me and Wayne are a couple, and I don't care who you are, if your husband or boyfriend gives you money to go shopping, then you go shopping. I don't think I'm different from any other girl in that way. I'm lucky because Wayne is a really generous person, he's not one of those boyfriends who keep tabs on you. He's never said, 'How much have you spent today?' Mind, we used to have joint credit cards and if you went over a certain limit the card would just stop and you wouldn't be able to use it. Normally, if I come back from the shops with a new dress or a bag, he never asks how much it cost. The only times he'll ever comment are while we're out shopping together, and he'll say something like, 'That's not worth the money.'

Wayne is different to me when it comes to shopping. He'll pick up a coat that's really expensive, maybe a few thousand pounds, and say, 'That's lovely, that.' I tell him it's not worth it but he'll just go ahead and buy it and he doesn't think twice about the price tag. If he likes it he'll get it, whereas I'm more aware of whether something is worth spending a lot of money on. If we are out shopping he might moan a bit, like any lad does when they are dragged round the shops. 'How many pairs of shoes do you need?' he'll say, or 'How many bags do you need?' That's his only moan, he never complains about the actual cost of something. Wayne's not a materialistic person. Also, he doesn't think about fashion in the same way as I do. I might be out wearing a brand-new outfit – bag, shoes, everything – and he won't know whether it's old, new or whatever.

If Wayne thinks I look nice he'll compliment me, but that's kind of rare. He just doesn't get as passionate about fashion and clothes as I do.

Reading this last chapter, it might well come across as if I don't care about money, but I'm never going to forget where I've come from and start taking things for granted. Both me and Wayne know we're really fortunate to earn the kind of income we do, which allows me to go shopping in designer stores, where I'm lucky enough to be able to afford things I like. We also understand that we're young and one day we won't be earning the same amounts as we're earning now. Footballers only have a short career, maybe up until their mid-thirties, and as for me, my career might be at its peak right now, I just don't know. I'm sure I'll always work, but I'm not always going to be on the front covers of magazines. At the moment, we have no responsibilities in terms of children, but once they come along then family will come first and we will provide for them. When that time comes I probably won't be buying every new designer handbag that comes out. Just the odd one!

chapter fourteen

pulling into a garage for petrol and an engagement ring

About a year after we first started seeing each other, me and Wayne got engaged on Monday 1 October 2003. It was romantic, but not exactly romantic in the traditional sense.

On the night itself, we were meant to be going out to a restaurant for a Chinese meal, but halfway there I decided I really didn't feel like it. So on the way back Wayne pulled into the garage, either to get some petrol or to use the cash machine, probably both. We were parked up when he reached inside his pocket and brought out this beautiful emerald-cut diamond engagement ring and asked me if I wanted to marry him. He was going to give it to me while we were having our meal, but he ended up proposing in the car. I didn't have to think about it. I said, 'Yeah, yeah, I do.'

On the way home, I telephoned my mum to tell her that we'd decided to come home for our tea and that we were engaged! When we arrived back she'd laid the table and had candles and a bottle of champagne out. A glass of champagne and a plate of my mum's corned-beef hash, sausage and beans, that was our engagement dinner! I couldn't think of a better way to celebrate. It was really lovely and I wouldn't have wanted it any other way.

To be honest, it wasn't the biggest surprise when Wayne proposed. He'd been talking about it for quite a while, but I was a bit unsure. I was only seventeen, and at the time I think I was worried about whether I was a little too young. But then I thought, no. I couldn't imagine being with anyone other than Wayne for the rest of my life. After all, I knew I was going to get engaged to him someday, so age didn't need to come into it. I'd already told Wayne that, so he knew that whenever he did decide to propose I was definitely going to say yes. What I didn't know was exactly when or where he was going to ask me.

Relaxing with Wayne at the England hotel during the World Cup.

Mind you, he gave me a big clue. Wayne's terrible at keeping secrets so I'd known for weeks that he'd been having a ring made specially for me by a jeweller because he hadn't stopped talking about it! Still, I never actually saw it until that night in the car on the garage forecourt.

Last year, Wayne bought me a new ring with an even bigger diamond. I don't know exactly how much he paid for it, but it's really special and both rings mean a lot to me, which is why that newspaper story about me and Wayne splitting up and me throwing my ring into the squirrel park by our old house was so ridiculous.

Me and my man at my twentieth birthday party.

The newspapers saw me without my ring one day and just concocted this big lie. I'd never do something like that because being engaged to Wayne means so much to me.

My mum and dad always knew how much Wayne meant to me and how strong our relationship was, so when they learned of our engagement they were really happy for us both. Being too young was never an issue for them. After all, my mum was only eighteen years old when she married my dad. I suppose me and Wayne felt the same way as they did about being together. If you know it's right then it doesn't matter how old you are. Not that my dad didn't feel like he was losing his little girl a bit. I'm equally close to both my mum and dad, and I can tell them everything, but I suppose that, compared to some girls, I've got a really good relationship with my dad.

If you know it's right then it doesn't matter how old you are. Not that my dad didn't feel like he was losing his little girl a bit.

I think maybe because I was their first and I'm a girl, dad's always been very protective towards me. If ever I went to town on a night out with my mates, my dad would always drive in to pick me up and take me home. I could understand why, but sometimes, when my mates were going off later to parties and stuff, I wished he was a little bit more relaxed. Having said that, it was good because I never had to go looking for a taxi, and my mates never used to complain. They'd be sorting out who was going to get a lift home with Coleen's dad and they used to love the fact that he'd pick us all up and stop off at the chippy on the way home. Even now he's wary about me getting into taxis on my own, in case someone's going to run off with me or something! If I'm getting a cab from Croxteth I'll make sure I always use the firm that my mate's dad runs. Dad was, still is, protective of me, but that's a good thing and I like to know he's looking out for me.

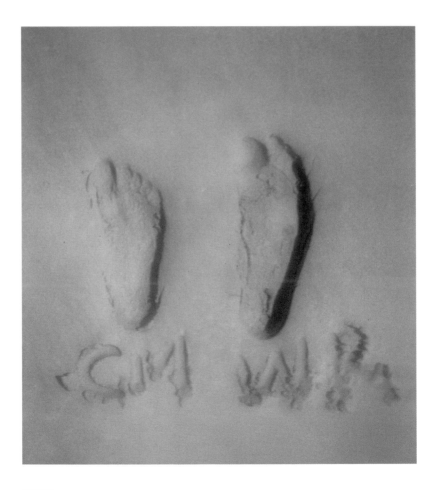

However, because of the way my dad cared for me, I think it might have been a bit hard for him to readjust to me growing up all of a sudden. I'm sure he never expected himself to allow Wayne to start living at our house, but it says a lot about the kind of person he is that he knew what the two of us meant to each other and it didn't become a problem. Actually, Wayne never officially moved in and brought his gear round. What happened was that his mum and dad had moved house, a bit further away, so he was spending most of the time round at our place. He didn't really move in, but, then again, he might as well have done! While he was there we didn't sleep in the same bedroom or anything. It was only after we'd moved out and bought our own house that we were allowed to do that.

When Wayne asked me to marry him, it did make a difference to our relationship. I know that sounds obvious, but being engaged gives you that extra bond. It just took us that little step

Like The Beatles said, 'All you need is love'. Here are my five reasons why:

Love is family.
Love is friendship.
Love is always being there, no matter what.
Love is trust.
Love is making people happy when they are down.

further. But, while I say that, there are some things it doesn't alter because we have such a strong relationship anyway. Being engaged is simply the natural step towards marriage and the future.

The experiences we've been through together, both personally and in our careers, have forced us to grow up quicker than a lot of couples our age. Going through all we have done has only brought us closer.

As far as marriage is concerned, we never thought we'd have a wedding straight away. My attitude now is the same as it was then. I don't think there's a need to rush into things, and when the time is right it'll come.

In the meantime, it's great to grow up together. Wayne has not changed an awful lot since we first met. He's still shy in some situations and he's still as cheeky as he always was. The main difference is that he's more mature about things compared to how he used to be. But that's only natural. Every lad's a bit mad when they're younger.

The experiences we've been through together, both personally and in our careers, have forced us to grow up quicker than a lot of couples our age. Going through all we have done has only brought us closer. I've been there from the beginning for Wayne, and likewise he was there for me, and we've helped each other along the way. I've learned from the good and bad things he's been through, and now he's learning from my career. We've both made mistakes along the way, but I always think mistakes happen for positive reasons. They are life's stepping stones.

Nothing compares to being with someone you know you want to spend the rest of your life with. Wayne was a friend in the beginning, before we ever started going out together. Now we're best friends, and that's the most important thing in our relationship.

chapter fifteen

the tears of leaving home & the house of our dreams

When me and Wayne moved into our first house, I cried non-stop for two weeks. We'd been living at my family home in Croxteth and that had been great, but by the end of 2003 we decided to get a place of our own. At first, we were going to get a flat, but then it looked like Wayne was going to stay at Everton long-term so instead we went for a house. Having viewed a load of properties, we eventually found this lovely detached house by the sea in Formby. Formby is a quiet coastal town, just on the border of Liverpool and close to Southport. The motorway is nearby, so a few of Wayne's team-mates from Everton lived there, including Duncan Ferguson and Alan Stubbs, as well as a few other footballers from Liverpool.

Looking back now, it was a bit mad. I was seventeen years old and had just left school and Wayne was only eighteen. We were at an age when, under normal circumstances, we'd be moving into a rented one-bedroom flat, if we were lucky, and here we were buying this one-million-pound house.

It was amazing. The house had four bedrooms, all with en suite bathrooms. Then there was an indoor swimming pool, which was just crazy when you think about it. We bought furniture and then I

Coleen: welcome to my world

set about decorating the place. I could have got an interior designer in to give me ideas, but I'd left school, wasn't really doing anything and I wanted to have a go myself, so the design and decorations were left to me. It was a time when I was experimenting with my clothes and everything, and I think that was reflected in my choices in interior design.

Looking back now, it was a bit mad. I was seventeen years old and had just left school and Wayne was only eighteen. We were at an age when, under normal circumstances, we'd be moving into a rented one-bedroom flat, if we were lucky, and here we were buying this one-million-pound house.

In the beginning, I had the idea of decorating every room in a different theme. However, in the end I went for pretty normal colours for most of the house. But as much as I loved the house I never fell in love with living there and being away from Croxteth and Liverpool. Those first two weeks were the worst, when I just couldn't stop crying. It's not that I didn't want to move, but I hated the fact it felt like we were so far away from home and everyone. Even now, the one thing I hate is being on my own. That's why me and Wayne both spend so much time at my mum's house, because we like being around people. That's the way my home has always been, a full house, surrounded by family and friends, where there's always something going on and someone to talk to. But there we were in this beautiful big house in Formby, in this lovely area, and all I could think about was that I knew nobody nearby and there was only us two living there. My mum and dad's house was only half an hour away down the motorway, but in my head it seemed like miles and miles.

I felt so young in some ways, which I suppose I was. I'd only just left school and we were living in this really big house. Even inviting friends round and being the hostess seemed weird.

It was great when friends and family came up to stay, but the problem was that we didn't really know people around us, neighbours or anyone, whereas before, in Croxteth, we knew everyone. The way I've always been, even now, is that when a mate's mum and dad go away on holiday everyone goes and lives in their house for two weeks, because you can have parties and do whatever you want. Now my mates lived so far away that they couldn't pop round like they normally would have done. They had to drive to get to us, and most of them didn't have a licence.

I felt so young in some ways, which I suppose I was. I'd only just left school and we were living in this really big house. Even inviting friends round and being the hostess seemed weird. I'd say, 'Are you coming round to ours?', but 'ours' had always been my mum and dad's house. Before, my friends would come round to 'ours' and mum would be there to make them a cup of tea or give them a biscuit. Then, all of a sudden, 'ours' was mine and Wayne's house and mates would come to visit and I literally didn't know

what to do. Should I cook them something to eat? What should I offer them? It was those little things that I couldn't get used to. When your mum's there, you'll ask whether someone wants a cup of tea and it appears. Perfect. But I don't drink tea or coffee. I knew how to make it, but I never knew how much milk to put in because I didn't know how people liked it. That sounds silly, doesn't it? But I was so young and everything was so new.

I used to go back to my mum's house, and when it came to going home, to my new home in Formby, I used to cry for the length of the journey.

In the end, we lived in Formby for 18 months before Wayne moved clubs. Eventually we found the house we live in now, but in between we spent time in one of Man United's club houses and a hotel.

Our home now can only be described as my dream house and I couldn't be happier. By the time we left Formby, Wayne had moved to Manchester United, so we wanted to buy somewhere close to their training ground. In the end, around about Christmas-time in 2005, we found a house set in two acres of land in a quiet village in Cheshire, where quite a few of the Man United players live. It wasn't really the house we fell for, it was more the possibilities of what we could do with it. The previous owners had already received planning permission to knock down the existing house, which meant we could build our own dream home from scratch. It took a while – I'm sure I've still got boxes of shoes in the garage – but finally, after over a year, I felt like we'd properly moved in and got it exactly how we wanted it. This time around, because we were a bit older and I had more work commitments, we decided to get an interior designer in to help with the décor.

One of the things me and Wayne have always said is that where we live now is our private home and our sanctuary away from the press and the public spotlight. We said right from the start that we didn't think we would ever do any of those 'at home' photo-shoots with the likes of *OK!* or *Hello!*, or allow journalists or TV reporters inside. When your life is lived in the public eye you want somewhere to escape to, which is yours and yours alone, something to keep for yourself, your family and your friends. So you won't see us doing one of those *Through the Keyhole* or MTV *My Crib* programmes anytime soon.

Where we live is a quiet area anyway with a private house on one side, a nursing home on the other, and a golf course to the rear. Every now and again we have a few kids standing outside asking for autographs, but that's very rare and nothing like the attention we had in Liverpool.

One of the things me and Wayne have always said is that where we live now is our private home and our sanctuary away from the press and the public spotlight.

The house itself isn't surrounded by barbed-wire fences or anything, but obviously security is an issue, especially because you hear of so many break-ins. Just in case anyone gets any ideas, we have CCTV cameras that monitor the house and garden and a security alarm system that's triggered by sensors and is linked directly to the local police station. There have been a few times when my brother has driven round when we've been out and let himself in, and the next thing I know

I've got a call from the police asking whether we know this person. At our other house in Formby we had nothing like that security-wise, but as you get older you become more conscious about these kinds of things.

Not that we ever want to be locked or hidden away from real life. Both me and Wayne are always aware of where we've come from, and we go home enough to our mum and dad's houses to never lose touch with that normality. Nor are we the kind of people who ever want to lose touch with our roots. We never take things for granted. From the Everton first team to the England team to the move to Manchester United, with Wayne's work, and now my work, everything has been a gradual stepping stone to where we are now. Well, gradual in terms of this accelerated life we're living. But everything that's happened, moving from my mum's to the house in Formby to the bigger house now, owning a Ka, then a Ford Focus, then up to the Bentley I'm driving which Wayne bought me for Christmas, it's all been equally as exciting. I don't want to lose that feeling of excitement.

We never take things for granted. From the Everton first team to the England team to the move to Manchester United, with Wayne's work, and now my work, everything has been a gradual stepping stone to where we are now.

When I was younger, I never imagined in my wildest dreams that I'd be living in the kind of house we live in now. I never imagined I'd drive the car I'm driving or all the lovely things I'm lucky enough to afford. Every now and again I have to pinch myself.

Wayne thinks the same way as well. Sometimes he'll sit in our living room and say, 'I can't believe it.' It's hard to imagine that just a few years ago we were still living at my mum and dad's house. Some days we just get on with it, but then there will be other times when we have people round who've never seen the house before, and we get such a buzz from their reactions and feel so proud.

One of the best things about our lives right now is being able to share it all with the people we love and care about. When you're surrounded by other people, that's when you really appreciate everything.

One summer we had a few friends – Wayne's brothers Graeme and John, and a few of his cousins – round for a barbecue, and everyone was partying until we ended up in the swimming pool. We look around and there's this bunch of mates who've grown up together in Croxteth, known each other for ages, and here we are messing about in this swimming pool in a big house in Cheshire that belongs to us. We're just a bunch of kids. I think it's mad but at the same time it's so lovely.

Maybe I was too young to move to the house in Formby. I probably wasn't quite ready. However, as I've got older I've started to appreciate my own space and enjoy the quiet times. Mind you, it is lovely when our families come round. Apart from the fact it's great having Mum and Dad round for dinner, she'll start fussing and putting our washing in the machine and doing stuff here and there. I tell her that we've got a cleaner so she really doesn't need to do all that, but mums can't help themselves and she likes it. And I like it too.

chapter sixteen

when the world isn't watching

I'm sure there are people who imagine we live this fabulous lifestyle with servants at our beck and call, and celebrities popping over for dinner every other night. The reality couldn't be further from the truth and that's just the way we like it. There's our life outside our home, where Wayne plays football in front of 70,000 fans every week and I get to do fantastic, glamorous photo-shoots, and then there's our life away from the spotlight. When we're at home alone we are no different from any other young couple who live together. We have a laugh, we sometimes argue, we sometimes irritate each other. I have my bad habits, Wayne has his, so we're normal. And it's that normal part of our life that I love more than anything else.

If I were to describe a typical night in for me and Wayne then I'd choose a Monday. That's because it's the one night of the week when Wayne will usually have played a match at the weekend so he'll be allowed to relax at home before the next game. He'll come back from the training ground at about 2.30 p.m., and then, if I haven't got anything in for tea, I'll go out and get something from one of the local supermarkets. Wayne has breakfast and lunch at the Man United training ground.

If I'm going to cook, then it'll more than likely be spaghetti bolognaise, chicken pasta, fish or salad. Depending on what we've been doing at the weekend, or whether Wayne has a match coming up midweek, we might have the odd glass or two of sauvignon blanc. Then it's a night in front of the telly.

I'll watch the football if there's a big match on, but otherwise I'm not usually that bothered unless Wayne's playing.

We call Monday nights 'Mad Monday' because we'll watch *Emmerdale*, *Coronation Street*, *EastEnders*, then *Corrie* again – that's our night in, watching the soaps. Wayne never used to watch them, but I think I've converted him into a fan. We've got Sky+ now, which is great. So sometimes we'll tape all the soaps and watch them after the football match. I'll watch the football if there's a big match on, but otherwise I'm not usually that bothered unless Wayne's playing. Wayne, on the other hand, will watch every football match going if you let him, whether it be the Italian league, Spanish league, you name it. If he can't find one of those he'll go through the channels until he finds a Chinese match or something. Sometimes he goes too far and I'll moan, and then one of us might go into another room to watch whatever we want. I like things like *Britain's Next Top Model*. If there's nothing on or I'm not doing anything then I'll go to bed around ten or half-past. I like my sleep. If I've had a big weekend I can easily go to bed at 9.30 p.m. and get up ten or eleven hours later.

Wayne is more likely to sit and watch a film for a couple of hours or maybe have a game on his computer. He likes his gadgets, but tends to keep getting something new, like an iPod, or a new game, or like the pinball machine in our games room, and he'll go through phases of playing things nonstop then get bored and not touch them for ages. I know him and the rest of the Man United team will go into each other's hotel rooms when they're away and play computer games, but he doesn't do it so much when he's at home. I'm not into stuff like that and, apart from the soaps, I'm not much of a telly person. I'd rather sit there and have a conversation with someone than watch the box.

When Wayne eventually comes up to bed he'll climb in and stick the fan on. No, not because it's hot. It doesn't matter what the season is or what the weather's like outside, there is always a fan stood next to our bed and Wayne can't get to sleep without it being switched on all night. It used to be the Hoover when he was a kid. Maybe you've read that story somewhere else already about how he falls asleep in the afternoon with the vacuum cleaner on. I kind of understand it. When I was a baby, my mum says I was just the same. If I wouldn't get off to sleep, she used to turn the vacuum on and I'd be dead to the world. I think with Wayne it goes back to his mum vacuuming while she was pregnant. Maybe it's a Liverpool thing – my mum's always got the Hoover out.

Nowadays it's the fan or the hairdryer that helps Wayne sleep and he rarely gets the vacuum out any more. Even when we are away and staying in a hotel, I'll come back from shopping and he'll be lying there fast asleep holding the hairdryer, which will be going on a cool setting. He rarely uses the hairdryer when I'm at home but he'll take it with him when he's staying away with Manchester United. I don't think he needs it, really, it's just a habit he's got into. There have been times when he's been travelling with the team and

I've seen him packing it away into his suitcase. I'll go, 'What are you doing with that hairdryer?', and he'll say it's to do his hair. 'It's not!' I'll say. 'I know what it's for!'

These days, just to keep the peace, I've got used to the fan going all night. In the beginning it used to irritate me and one night I hid it away and he was searching all over till he eventually found where it was. But now I don't mind. It's not too bad to put up with. I'm sure if you asked Wayne there would be things I do that irritate him. Top of his list would be me keeping him awake by grinding my teeth through the night.

Nothing Wayne does really gets on my nerves ... Perhaps I can think of a couple of things, like the way he's constantly biting his nails right down – I don't know what he does with the nails he's bitten off. The other one is the way he takes centre stage at parties with his dance flips and routines. Actually, that does my head in! Sometimes when there's a big circle of people he'll invite me in there and then he'll be lifting me up in the air. One time, at a friend's birthday party, he was asking me to come over into the middle and I just stormed off!

Not that I don't like dancing. I love it if I'm in a good mood. If I'm bored or Wayne's got a cob on, I'll just dance around the house trying to cheer him up. I don't even need music. I'll bounce around the living room all over the sofa trying to make him laugh. Sometimes it works and sometimes it doesn't!

Since we moved into our new house, we've tried to be tidier than we naturally are. We have a cleaner and gardener who both come in and help out. We found the gardener and window cleaner through Manchester United, and I think Janet, our cleaner, was employed by our management company. Everyone who works for us has to sign a confidentiality agreement. I know that sounds a little bit over the top and paranoid, but you're always hearing stories of housekeepers and nannies selling their stories to the tabloids these days so you can't be too careful.

Since we moved into our new house, we've tried to be tidier than we naturally are.

Janet comes in five days a week for a couple of hours. She'll do the bathrooms, mop the floors, put the washing in and stuff. It is a privilege to have someone do all that for you. It's nice to leave the place in the morning and come back to a clean house and everything's done. Not that I leave it in a tip, but I might leave the dishes out or something. When I lived at home we'd help out with the washing-up and always put our clothes by the washing machine, but I've never really done ironing or the usual household chores. I know, I'm lucky!

We've got the granny flat by the side of the house so we can have a housekeeper if we need one. I think, in the future, if we moved to a bigger house, we'd get a housekeeper, but at the moment I don't think I'd like someone living in.

Then again, there are times when I do think I would like a house-keeper. I'm fairly tidy but Wayne is just a mess. No, maybe that's unfair. Ever since we moved into this house he's been good. Before, at night, or whenever he'd step out of his clothes, he'd just leave them on the floor, but now he'll either put them in the corner or in the washing basket or take them down to the laundry. I'm just as bad really. If I'm going on a night out my room ends up in a right state, because I try loads of clothes on and never put them back. We do try, though. I probably make more of a mess at mum's house than I do at my own. Once you get your own house I think you make more of an effort.

That's why when I invite my mates over I tell them there can't be any parties. I'll have a night when we'll all have a drink but it's nothing like when their mums and dads go away. Why? I'm not getting my house messed up. Once they all get drunk, they just don't care and start doing whatever they want!

But we do have friends round. As I mentioned earlier, Wayne's two brothers, his cousins and three of my friends came over for a barbecue once. We were sitting out in the garden until the early hours of the morning and all of a sudden it started raining. We all ran in, leaving the food on the table, then it went on all night and there was a right mess. We woke up the next day and there were burgers floating everywhere. It was just disgusting.

One time we had a few friends round for dinner and hired caterers to come in and do everything. We'd been round to one of Wayne's friends and they'd done something similar, so we thought it would be nice. And it was lovely, but it does feel a bit weird when you have these strangers in your home cooking and serving and doing everything for you.

I think Wayne would like to have a few dogs around the place but I don't want any animals. Apart from anything else, we are not at home enough so it wouldn't be very fair. We have had dogs in the past, though, and I grew up with them. When I was a kid we used to have a boxer called Rocky who was about eleven when he died. Then I had a Westie called Casper, who was only one and a half years old when he was knocked over outside our house. After that, we stopped having them because it was too upsetting when they died.

But then while we were living at my mum and dad's, Wayne bought me a chow named Fizz, and later on I bought a white fluffy bichon frise called Daisy, but because we've moved backwards and forwards over the past few years they now both live at Mum's.

Not that our attempts at owning a dog stopped there. I bought Wayne a black chow called Bella in the summer whilst we were living in the house at Formby. However, not long after Wayne moved to Manchester United, for a little while we moved to my auntie and uncle's house with Bella. In fact, they ended up buying Bella's sister from the same litter. Shortly we were on the move again – firstly to a hotel and then a club-rented house. So we left Bella with them and she's been there ever since. Bella and her sister got on so well, we didn't want to split them up. It's complicated but I don't think we should get any more dogs.

As far as pets go, I'm happy with the rabbits and squirrels in the garden and the odd badger and fox that we see wandering around. If I want anything more exotic then I can go round to my mum and dad's house. They've still got the terrapin, Jack, that my uncle bought me when I was one year old. There were two, Jack and Jill, but Jill fell down the hill, so to speak, and died when she was young. But Jack's going strong and he's massive. Then there's Bob, the talking parrot. He says all sorts, like, 'Rooney

244   Coleen: welcome to my world

Goal', or he'll go 'Coleen' then he'll give out a wolf whistle! Charming. I don't know who taught him that.

No, I don't think we're going to get any pets in the near future. Our lives are here, there and everywhere at the minute and we're happy to spend the free time we have together on our own. And, to be honest, I think looking after ourselves is a big enough responsibility to deal with right now!

chapter seventeen

my experience of men and fashion … i.e. wayne

I can't pretend to be an expert on men's fashion. I take an interest, but given that I'd never really had a boyfriend before Wayne and he doesn't really follow fashion, my experience is quite limited in that area. My brothers are into their clothes, but Wayne is not really that fashion-conscious. I will buy him clothes, though, and point out things that I'd like him to wear, but I'm not the kind of girlfriend who'll go out and style their boyfriend from top to bottom. Wayne's Wayne and I wouldn't change him.

To be honest, I don't think I'd be attracted to a lad who was too into themselves and the way they look. I could never go out with the pretty-boy type.

Not that Wayne's lack of fashion knowledge stops him from sometimes thinking he's being really fashionable. Whether it's cars or clothes he likes the idea of being different from everyone else and having something nobody else has. So, say with cars, he bought one of those big Chryslers, but as soon as the same model was widely available then he wanted to sell it.

That's fine with cars, only sometimes, when he's been impulse-buying, his choice of clothes isn't nearly as tasteful and I'll tell him so. One day he came home having bought this big red leather jacket with a black and white design across the shoulders, from a shop in Wilmslow near where we live. It was, to be blunt, a right show, but he thought it was boss! He only wore it a couple of times, thankfully. Maybe that was because in the end I hid it and he never asked for it again.

I reckon that part of the reason Wayne's always looking to be the first and different to everyone else is the influence of the Manchester United dressing room. While Wayne might not really compete in the fashion stakes the way some of the other lads do occasionally he does like to go in of a morning and show off his new shoes or jacket.

> The lads like to compete and they'll skit each other something awful if they see one of the players turning up in a jumper or a jacket they don't like the look of.

One year, Wayne decided to grow a beard. It was at the start of the season when he wasn't playing that well and the rumour on the terraces was that he wasn't going to cut his beard off until he scored a goal. That wasn't the reason at all. There was no reason – he just hadn't shaved. Although in the past he has had little joke competitions with his friends about who can grow their hair or beard the longest. Daft things like that.

My experience of men and fashion … i.e. Wayne   **249**

Wayne is different from me in that instead of buying new clothes throughout the year he'll go out in winter and do a big shop. Usually, he goes to Flannels in Manchester, or Cricket, where he'll choose a load of gear and spend a fortune in one go. Then, now and again, he'll ask me to go to Cricket and pick out some clothes for him. Cricket's good because they will let you take the clothes home, try them on there and bring them back if they're not right. It makes it a whole lot easier, otherwise there's always a load of press outside the door when he's shopping.

When I'm choosing stuff for Wayne I never go for anything over the top. In the main it will be classic and smart-casual gear like jumpers, T-shirts, jeans or just basic shoes.

Last time I found him some D Squared jeans, but they can be a bit tight in the leg. Tight isn't really a good look on Wayne. Because of the football, he's got quite big thighs. So, next time around, I got him a pair of Dior jeans. In fact I picked up quite a bit of Dior – a black cardigan, a V-neck jumper in beige, a plain polo shirt and then two Prada shirts. He was happy. He likes his designer brands. He's not much of a trouser-wearer but he's got loads of jeans – Hugo Boss, Blue Blood, True Religion, that kind of thing. I also like popping into some of the high-street stores for Wayne. Top Man, Reiss and Gap do some really good pieces. I have also brought him stuff home from George at Asda. However, mostly he likes wearing his tracksuits, which are ideal for him to go to and from training. He has loads of Nike as they're one of his main sponsors.

One for the boys

Admittedly, I might not be the world's biggest expert on men's styling, but even I know that your man need only make one or two additions to his wardrobe to transform him from fashion flop to cool dude. Next time he goes into town, slip the following list into his pocket:

A crisp white shirt

Clean, classic and narrow-cut, a man can't fail to look impressive.

A cashmere sweater

Available on the high street and not nearly as expensive as they used to be, whether it be round neck, or a roll neck, worn with a shirt or without.

Dark blue denim jeans

No rips, patches, frays or paint drips allowed. Can be worn anywhere and with anything on his feet.

A wool coat

Go for a knee-length, single-breasted Crombie or pea coat for classic modern British style with rock-star attitude.

A smart pair of leather shoes

Maybe brogues. Nothing too pointy or square, to give him a touch of the English gent.

A slim-fitting single-breasted suit

All men look the business in a good suit.

When it comes down to it, Wayne gets more excited about watches than clothes. He's not really into jewellery as such, he hasn't got his ears pierced or anything, but he's into his watches – buying them for himself and me. Right now, I'd say his favourites are a Franck Muller and a Daytona. I bought him one by New York's Jacob for his twentieth birthday. It has two faces that can be alternated and one of them has a map of the world fashioned out of diamonds. I call it his 'bling watch'! He liked it so much I had another one custom-made by Jacob for his twenty-first birthday.

I know that these days some footballers have a reputation for fancying themselves a bit, and concentrating more on their appearance than their game, but that will never apply to Wayne.

Not that he doesn't take care of himself, but he's not into things like waxing his chest. I've tried to encourage him to do more by buying him creams and moisturizers by Kiehl's and loads of different Lancôme products, only he'll go through phases of using them and never stick at it. He started using face scrubs for a while but he never keeps to a routine. He hasn't got a massive vanity case that he takes to the training ground every morning. If he did then probably the only thing in it would be aftershaves – Armani, Hugo Boss and Sean Jean's Unforgivable, which I really like.

At this moment in time I cannot see Wayne getting over-interested in fashion or bringing out his own aftershave, but you never know. As much as Wayne loves new clothes he's not one for flicking through men's magazines and following this season's trends. Wayne's Wayne, and I'm happy about that.

chapter eighteen

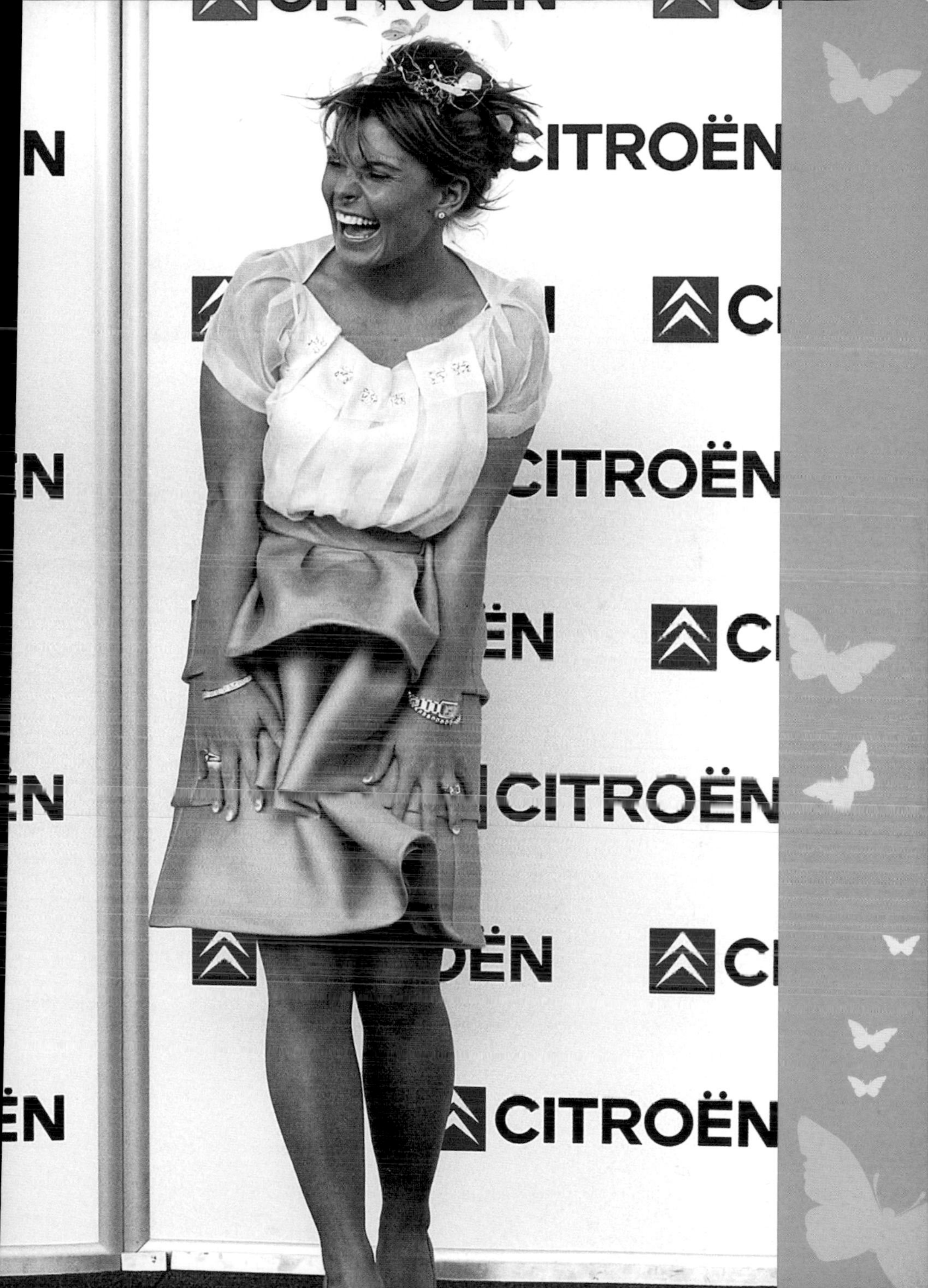
CITROËN
CITROËN
CITROËN
CITROËN

eyes and teeth: if they're smiling then so's the rest of you

I'm not one of those girls who lives in the mirror, but when it comes to beauty and maintenance I do like to take care of myself. After all, I'm not going to be twenty-one forever. And I'm a girly-girl, and though I'm not big on make-up I can't resist a new lotion or potion.

Every now and again my mates and I will have a girly night in and I'll light candles, open up a bottle of wine and we'll all sit around with facemasks on. I've got some really funny photos of us all sat there of an evening, looking like something from another planet! I love my girly nights in. We'll do family ones as well. My mum has five sisters and every so often all my aunties and all my cousins will make a night of it round my mum's. There will be about twenty or more of us in total, Mum will do some food, organise drinks, and we won't shut up talking all night. It's a really nice time – when we all get together. We have a good laugh and sometimes a singsong. Other nights, my mum will also arrange for Emma, the girl who does our nails, to come round and pamper us. Sometimes we will just have a chat and a few glasses of wine – either way it's a great night.

My philosophy on beauty is that if you practise the basics now then you'll reap the benefits in the long run, a bit like Wayne and the effort he puts into training! I'd never become obsessive about it, but being in the spotlight and having to go on photo-shoots and events as part of my job I've become more aware of my skincare routine and how I look after myself. Mind, I don't think I'd be any different if all that wasn't part of my life. From skincare to hair to treatments to waxing, here's my beauty routine:

Skincare – too much is too much

When I was fourteen or fifteen years old I used to suffer from spots. Not big spots with heads on, but I used to get these spots underneath the skin on my forehead, though it wasn't as bad as the acne or the boils that some kids at school were unlucky enough to have. However, naturally, I hated them, and you know yourself that it's not right. My mum and dad took me to the doctor's loads of times and he said it was a form of acne, then prescribed me with loads of creams and tablets and face-washes. None of them seemed to work. In the end, my mum and dad paid for me to go to see a private dermatologist and he put me on a tablet called Roaccutane. It's a very strong tablet. They only give it to a few people because its effects are so intense – there has even been talk in the newspapers about it causing depression, but that wasn't my experience. What it does do is dry all your skin out, even your lips. Thankfully, by the time I'd taken the full course it had cleared my skin and the spots have never come back since.

I understand that this kind of skin problem can affect kids when they're at school, but I never let it bother me. It didn't make me depressed or anything. I think of myself as quite a confident person and I never let spots alter that. I just wanted to get rid of them.

I don't mind telling people that my skin was bad, because I think it's something that everyone worries about. I've been on photo-shoots and the make-up artists have commented on how nice my skin is and I tell them it never used to be like that. I think that if I came through that stage in life then everyone can. My brothers Joe and Anthony have suffered the same as me, but thankfully theirs have gone away as well.

Nowadays, my skincare routine involves alternating creams because that's meant to be better for you. I use a lot of YSL skincare products – moisturizer, cleanser and toner – at the moment, but I'll change every now and again. Right now, I've been switching between YSL and Guinot. However, of all the products I use, the one I go for every time is Johnson's three-in-one wipes. They are really good and I'm always telling everyone to use them. On some days I'll put cleanser and toner on, but with Johnson's wipes I'll just wash my face and moisturize. Occasionally I might use a Dermalogica face wash – it's a really nice face scrub. Dermalogica also do a lovely eye cream that I'll use every now and again, particularly on the morning after a big weekend or a night out.

Like most girls, my skin ranges from being quite dry to normal, depending on my time of the month. I've never worn a lot of make-up, and quite a lot of the time I'll go for days without wearing any make-up at all. There are times when I can't be bothered with all my creams and I'll get up, wash my face and that's me done. You can spend a fortune on all kinds of treatments, but I think, at the end of the day, the best therapy is to give yourself a break from all the treatments now and again and allow the pure fresh air to get to your skin.

Hair – anything but a full fringe

I've had hair extensions in and out since I was seventeen years old. Usually, I'll take them out when we go away on holiday to give my hair a rest. My hair is naturally quite fine and when I was younger I used to have a bob, which made it seem thicker than it was. When I tried to grow it longer my hair never had the fullness I wanted. I knew a few girls in Liverpool who'd had extensions done so in the end I booked into a salon called Herbert's in Liverpool city centre and I've been going there ever since.

If you've got extensions then it's really important to take care of them. My hair is braided first and then the extensions are sewn in, and I'll go to the salon every four or five weeks to have them taken out, re-sewn and tightened. Nowadays, I'm so used to having my hair the way it is that whenever I take them out it feels like I'm bald!

I get my extensions done at Herbert's, although sometimes I also go to Wayne's cousin Leanne who's also really good, and my colour and cut at the Barbara Daly salon in Liverpool, by a great stylist called Liza. If I've got an event on, an awards dinner for instance, I'll book in to see Liza. Or if it's at the weekend, like the Beckhams' party, she might come to my house.

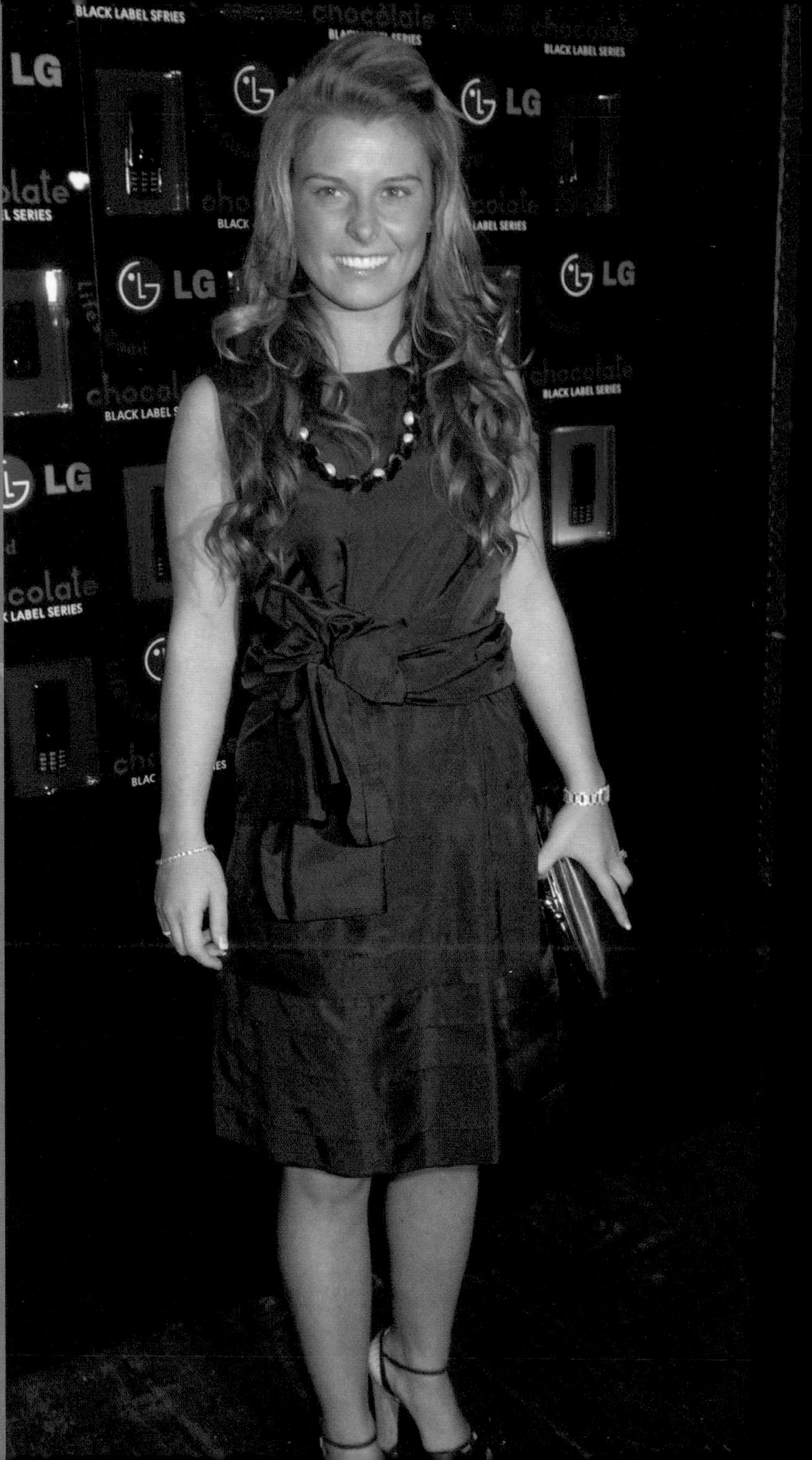
BLACK LABEL SERIES
LG
chocolate
BLACK LABEL SERIES

I'm naturally brown-haired and first had highlights put in when I was sixteen and I had just started seeing Wayne. It was quite a big deal, because I'd wanted them done for ages and my mum had always told me to wait until I was older. (Up until the age of sixteen I had my hair cut by the same hairdresser who used to come to the house to do my mum's.) My mum and dad are always ones for saying that the natural look suits me best. Whenever I mention my extensions at home my dad will always go, 'I don't know why you can't have your own hair, Coleen!' I suppose he's right in a way. Natural is always best, but I like my blonde highlights. I've gone even lighter of late, but now I'm returning more and more to my natural colour.

One thing I really enjoy is going to the hairdresser's for a blow-dry every week. I could sit there all day letting Liza play with my hair, I just find the process relaxing. There's nothing more soothing than having your hair washed by someone else and having a little head massage at the end of it. Oh, I could fall asleep right now just thinking about it! At the salon they use a shampoo and conditioner called Kerastase and I'll use the same products at home, maybe together with a strengthening treatment. While on holiday I'll use a protection spray.

Normally, I like my hair off my face, just because I always feel fresher with it like that. I'll alternate, but for special dos I prefer it up. Not only because I feel better that way, but because you see so many girls wearing their hair down these days that it's nice to be different. That said, I'm really open to experimenting with all kinds of styles. Liza has a really good eye so I trust her to come up with something lovely. They keep a big book with loads of styles that they've either seen in magazines or on the catwalk, and every now and again we'll try something new out.

I went to the Heroes Awards in Liverpool and Liza gave me this 1960s style but with a ponytail. It looked great. She's so good that I usually allow her to do whatever she fancies. I once took a tear from a magazine and asked for something similar. That was when Sienna Miller was doing an ad campaign for Matthew Williamson and she had her hair in a band and combed back. It was lovely and I wanted to try it out.

Nature's way

If you fancy going for my natural make-up look then here are a few tips:

Apply a moisturizer with light reflective particles that will make your skin glow.

Use a very, and I mean very, sheer liquid foundation, and apply only where necessary rather than over the whole face.

Use a tinted lip gloss instead of lipstick for colour that looks sheer and natural.

Avoid using lots of powder. It makes the skin look older, I'm afraid.

Go for a pinky-coloured cream blusher. It gives the face a cute, childlike flush.

Use a very natural mascara. You're going for a glossy tint rather than thickening or curling.

Coleen: welcome to my world

I've tried loads of styles over the last few years – some good, some bad – but the one I don't think I would try again too soon is the full fringe. At the time I thought it was lovely, but on reflection perhaps it was not the right style for me.

At the moment I like my hair long, with natural colouring and a few blonde highlights. Lately, I've been trying to style it into a middle parting, just because it's a bit trendier, though it always seems to slide back to my usual side parting, so maybe that's not going to work out. If it was up to my stylist, I'd look totally different. She's been going on and on at me for ages to cut it short, and I've been resisting. When I was younger I had a short bob so I think it would suit me. Who knows what I'll have done next. I love trying new things. If you don't recognize me the next time I'm seen out in public, don't say I didn't warn you.

All eyes

The truth of the matter is, I'm blind! No, I can't say that, but my eyesight is quite bad. I started wearing glasses when I was seven, then I had my first set of contact lenses when I was around twelve or thirteen years old, which is quite young. When we went on holiday or to the swimming baths I used to have to take my glasses off, which meant I couldn't see a thing. I hated that. These days I use monthly contact lenses, but now I'm twenty-one I'm looking into correcting my eyesight with laser treatment. They say it's not recommended until you reach that age. Personally, I can't wait.

Apart from the effect it'll have on my sight, the last thing you want to do after a night out is to go through the rigmarole of taking your lenses out. I don't know how I manage it sometimes! Only once in the last few years have I forgotten. Usually, I'll wake up in the morning and because my eyesight's so bad everything is blurred. Then, this one time, I woke up and went, 'I can see! I can see!' Everything was as clear as day and I thought there had been some kind of miracle until I realized I'd left my lenses in overnight!

I've had my eyebrows waxed a couple of times but I prefer to pluck them myself. The last time I had them waxed the girl took the skin off because the wax was too hot and I ended up with a big cut. I've been put off ever since.

In terms of eye creams, I tend to use moisturizer. In the past I've tried anti-ageing creams, but products like Crème de La Mer and La Prairie are too rich for me at the moment and leave my skin quite greasy. Luckily, I don't have to worry about anti-ageing just yet.

As I've said before, my make-up is kept to a minimum and I'm not a lover of mascara. In fact, I hate mascara. The only time I ever wear mascara is when I know I've nothing in my diary for the next day, because no matter how much I try to wipe it off I'm always left with these black shadows around my eyes. If anything, I'd rather wear clear mascara. Other than that, I've tried eyelash extensions, glued on, but they only last a night on me and then I pull them off.

Oi! Referee! Beauty foul!

Unless you are going for a bit-part in the film version of *Footballers' Wives* there's no need, or excuse, for the following:

Getting lippy

Dark lip-liner is a complete no-no. Choose a liner that matches the colour of your lips and won't look unnatural.

Fake bake

A summery golden glow is great, but orange is, well, orange. Don't overdo the fake tan. Also limit those sunbed sessions. They quickly age the skin.

The Bronze Age is long gone

Too much bronzer can mean extremely unflattering streaky cheeks, and look as if you are still learning how to apply make-up.

Message in a bottle of peroxide

Hair that is too blonde just looks flat and has no depth.

Easy tweezy

Over-plucked eyebrows make your face look unbalanced and, to be honest, frightening!

Teeth and lips

There's nothing more beautiful than a smile. If I was asked to pick my best feature then I would say my teeth every time. I always think if you've got good teeth then you are more confident when you smile, and a smile really does make the rest of you look better. Best of all, a smile costs nothing. I know that's a cliché but it really is true.

I go for a regular six-month check-up at the dentist and have my teeth polished at the same time. I don't mind going to the dentist because we've always gone regularly since we were young. I reckon one of the reasons I've got good teeth now is because I've never been scared of the dentist's chair. When I was thirteen, I thought one of my front teeth was crossing over a bit and I was paranoid that as I got older it would get worse and worse. In the end, I asked the dentist for a brace. He said I didn't need one but I went on and on so much that he gave in and I ended up wearing a brace for six months. It was a time when loads of girls at school had braces so it never bothered me.

Only once have I tried whitening. My teeth are naturally white but the dentist said I could go another grade or two up and so I had this treatment that involved wearing a gum-shield that contained a whitening liquid. Arghhh! Never ever again! My teeth became so sensitive that I cried and cried the next day. Every time I opened my mouth the air would come in and my teeth would kill me. The next day I filled the gum-shield up with Sensodyne toothpaste and drove around like that all day. I'm really not sure how good whitening is for your teeth in the long term. I know I'll never do it again.

DIY home spa treatment

I've already mentioned the beauty nights I have with my mates, where we lounge around with face masks on consuming a few glasses of wine. Have a go at our home facial, which, if shared between a few of you, shouldn't worry your credit card too much and guarantees luxury spa results.

Step One: Use a make-up remover, paying particular attention to eye make-up.

Step Two: Deep-cleanse the skin with a cleanser. Spend a few minutes massaging the cleanser into the skin to ensure maximum effect.

Step Three: Get rid of dead skin cells using a gentle facial exfoliator. Dead skin cells make the complexion look dull and result in dry, flaky patches. For a DIY exfoliator try using oats mixed with a little water. It works!

Step Four: Apply a facemask according to your skin type. So 'deep cleansing' if your skin is oily or prone to clogged pores, 'moisturizing' if skin is dry, 'firming' if you are worried about fine lines or wrinkles.

Step Five: While you have the facemask on, apply an eye-mask to soothe and cool puffy eyes. For a DIY eye-mask use slices of cucumber or soaked chamomile teabags.

Step Six: After removing the mask, spend a few minutes massaging in your moisturizer, working from the neck up and outwards. The more blood flow through the skin the more you glow.

For me it's the more natural the better. I've never been one for lipstick really and I have always been into my lip-glosses. As far as looking after my lips goes I'll use a Dermalogica gel that's for both your eyes and lips, and I'll use Vaseline pretty much throughout the day to keep them moist. Then lip-balms and lip-glosses. I'm mad on them and could probably fill this book with a whole list. Right now, I swap between Dior, Chanel and Lancôme lip-glosses and the Juicy tubes. I also really love the lip-pump lip-gloss by Pout. It really does something to your lips.

Smooth legs

Maybe it's my eyebrow experience but I really don't like waxing at all. I've used hair-removal creams in the past and some are actually quite good, but right now I shave. Sometime soon I'm going to try out a laser hair-removal treatment.

Manicures and pedicures

I have had pedicures done in the past. Normally the girl who does my manicures also does my pedicures. Depending on what I feel like, I'll paint them whatever colour I fancy. I'm not really governed by trends.

I've had fingernail extensions for quite a while now, and every two weeks I'll go to get them redone and filled. I used to only get them done when I was going to a party or an event, but now I keep them on all the time. I like to keep the tips white but occasionally I'll paint them with a varnish or I'll get them done professionally. A girl called Vicky used to do them – she was really good – but now, for convenience, my manicurist Emma comes round to my mum's house.

Sun care – force yourself to be good

I'm the same as every girl, in that when I go on holiday I want to come back looking nice and brown, and so I'll put my hand up and say I never used to be as careful as I am now. I like a tan, so I'm afraid I'm not one of those girls who'll sit in the shade or under a parasol all day. Recently, though, I've been taking more care. I use Lancaster sun cream and start off with a factor 25 on my face and then work down to lower factors throughout the holiday. I'll go for an even higher factor on my body, depending on which country I'm in. Afterwards I'll moisturize with either Lancaster or Kiehl's, and of course I'll be using a lip-balm with UV protection throughout the holiday, to protect my lips.

I tend to tan quite easily and keep my colour for quite a long time after I come home, but when it does start to fade I top it up with a little bit of bronzer on my face.

A girl's little secret

I love my bed and I have good reason to. Beauty sleep really does exist. Overnight the skin repairs and replenishes itself, much better than during the day, helping it to lose that dull appearance and avoid dryness.

Treatments – treat yourself every now and again

There is pretty much nothing I won't try if I come out more relaxed and feeling better than I did when I went in. When I'm on holiday, I'm always having massages, and now and again my mates and I go to a spa.

Usually I'll go for a facial once a month. It's not something I put in the diary but I try to make it a regular date just to clear out my skin. In the past, I've tried loads of different types of facials, including the Crystal Clear facial, which involves this sucker-type machine that goes over your face and clears out your pores. You can really see the difference and your skin feels much fresher afterwards. My favourite, though, is the Hydradermie Facial. Your skin is cleansed, toned and moisturized, then this machine, which I can only describe as having small metal balls, vibrates across your skin. Sometimes when it goes over your teeth, and you've got a filling, you can taste the metal. I'm not so keen on that bit, but when you walk out you can feel the overall benefit.

What else have I tried? Well, I've been for body wraps but I don't really think much of them. It is hard to resist something that says you're going to lose six inches or so in one session, so I booked myself in just before we went on holiday. Having spent what seemed like ages wrapped in these cold, wet, clay bandages, I can't say I saw much difference apart from me getting very bored!

Other than massages, I also now and again have endermologie. I don't suffer from really bad cellulite but I have got bits and this treatment is meant to help. What happens is you wear a clear bodysuit and then the whole of your body is massaged up and down with a hand-held roller that contains a vibrating vacuum pump. It's meant to work on the cause of cellulite at a deep tissue level rather than simply on the surface, so it is quite hard on your skin. I'm no expert but I do know that after I've had it done I feel much better.

Like any other girl, I look at myself and see things that I'd like to change, but I'd never say I hated anything about myself. If I've got a spot I can't help squeezing and squeezing it until it's gone. I'd like to be able to see! I'd like thicker hair so I didn't have to wear extensions.

Oh, and if you really want to have a go at me then take a long, hard look at my nose. That's one thing I would change. I've got a bent nose! When I was about seven years old I used to constantly be twitching it – you know, like *Bewitched*, twitching it from side to side. My granddad used to tell me off and tell me to stop, otherwise, he said, I'd end up looking like Miss Piggy! He was right! If you look closely I've got one nostril that is bigger than the other and I've ended up with a nose that's slightly lopsided. If ever my brothers want to wind me up they say, 'B. N.' to me – Bent Nose. Or they'll say, 'Shut up, Bent Beak!' Nice! I'm not bothered. People have a lot worse wrong with them.

I've always said that beauty is to do with feeling good about yourself, and if you feel good about yourself then others will feel good about you.

Oh, and never forget to keep smiling. There isn't a treatment out there that can compete with a genuine smile.

chapter nineteen

beach babe

I could go on holiday every week of the year and wouldn't complain, but with the work commitments I have and with Wayne only getting a certain amount of time off when the season's finished, it's just not possible. Usually he's allowed about six or seven weeks in the summer, unless England are playing in the European Championships or the World Cup, when it can be as little as three weeks. We will go for weekend trips to the likes of Paris, and I try to get away with my friends during March, but unless Wayne is given time off by Manchester United we'll have one big summer holiday a year.

Since me and Wayne have been together we've been to some fantastic places – Barbados, Dubai, the French Riviera – and stayed in amazing hotels, including the only seven-star hotel in the world. We're a bit more used to travelling these days, but the same couldn't exactly be said of our first proper holiday together.

It was the summer of 2003 and we'd just been with all the England players, wives and girlfriends at a training camp/get-together in La Manga. Afterwards, we decided to go over to Miami, then on to Mexico, where we were going to be joined later by both our mums and dads.

Our agent booked the holiday for us. I know people think footballers are cosseted, that everything's done for them, and, to be honest, there's quite a lot of truth in that. I can't deny there's not something lovely about having someone looking after you and organizing your holidays, transport, all sorts. Still, I know we should really learn how to do things for ourselves a bit more because I realize it's not always going to be like this. Anyway, Paul organized the holiday for us and we flew straight to Miami.

A day at the beach. Point a camera at me and I'll smile!

We were only there for a few days and I've got to admit I thought it was a bit rubbish and the weather was bad. The drinking laws are really strict in America so unless you are twenty-one you can't go into a bar and you feel like you aren't allowed to do anything. So we'd stay in and get room service and argue with each other about things like who was going to tip the man who brought the food. Not about whose money it was, but who'd actually hand it over! We'd never done that kind of thing before, and we both felt self-conscious. When I look back now, we were so young and new to it all. We were only seventeen years old, it was our first holiday on our own, and we didn't know what to do.

The first few days in Mexico weren't much better. We'd been so used to going on holidays with our mums and dads and having things done for us, like organizing day trips, that we didn't realize you had to do that kind of stuff for yourselves!

Once our mums and dads came over it was miles better. They organized day trips and everything, and we ended up having a really good time. Well, that's not counting the time I almost drowned!

I was out swimming in the sea when I was dragged under by some freak waves. I'm a strong swimmer but even I couldn't cope. As much as I tried, I couldn't get back to shore and it felt as though I was going to drown. I started waving at everyone sitting on the beach to help me, and although it's funny to look back on it now, my dad thought I was waving and nothing was wrong, but I was drowning! Luckily, Wayne realized I wasn't all right and dived in after me, managing to pull me clear, minus my bikini, which had been pulled off by the strength of the waves! He really was my hero that day!

I've always loved family holidays. When I was growing up we were forever piling in the back of my dad's estate, sometimes as many as ten of us kids, including our cousins crammed into the boot, on a day trip to Llandudno or Haven. Some of my favourite times were those spent at our caravan in West Kirby, a coastal resort an hour or so from Liverpool. As little kids we'd come back from school on a Friday, have our tea, and mum would have us all in our pyjamas ready and waiting for dad to come home from work. Then we'd drive out of Liverpool, through the Birkenhead Tunnel and on to West Kirby. At the end of the journey we'd be straight off to bed ready for the next day.

Dad had bought the caravan for a couple of hundred pounds. You couldn't describe it as luxurious but we did it up nicely, painting the outside turquoise and beige, and fixing it up with new cushions and curtains that mum had arranged to get made specially. The kitchen was tiny with a little stove but I've seen my mum cook roast dinner on a Sunday lunchtime for twelve members of the family on that little stove. I don't know how she did it.

We used to have some great weekends over there. If it was hot we'd swim in the sea, mucking around, doing all sorts. There were horse stables nearby so we used to go out on hacks down the beach. When I was a bit older I would help out down the stables a little, mucking out and grooming the horses.

Of a Saturday night there was a club called The Hut, where bands would play and all the adults would bring their own ale because there wasn't a bar there. On Sunday mornings there would be a market and a car-boot sale. Not surprisingly, I used to love going round the car boot, buying loads of rubbish like broken old board games that we somehow found a use for and old bikes that people had left behind on the site.

West Kirby was great. Over time, some of my aunties and uncles, including my uncle Frankie who was the life and soul of the caravan park, ended up buying caravans there. My mum and dad still go across every now and then, although our turquoise and beige two-berth is long gone.

When we weren't holidaying in West Kirby, we'd be up the road in New Brighton or Rhyl, or we'd take a trip up to Blackpool to see the lights and go down to the Pleasure Beach.

Now and again, I still go across to Blackpool for a day out at the fair. I went with Wayne, my two brothers and their mates not long ago. It was a Monday night so the Pleasure Beach was dead and we had all the rides to ourselves. You can't beat Blackpool for a laugh.

Every other year or so we would go abroad for the summer. We went to Spain a couple of times, and then, when I was twelve, we went to Disneyland in Florida. That was dead exciting. My dad had discovered he had prolapsed discs in his back, which meant he wasn't able to be a bricklayer any more, so he took an early pension from the council. With the money we had the house done up a bit and then we went to Florida and were spoiled rotten. My dad would say, 'It's the Magic Kingdom, go on, get anything, get whatever you want!', and we would be in the shop grabbing all the Mickey Mouse pens and teddies and key rings, while my mum stood there with the trolley telling my dad off: 'Don't be saying that to them!' Disneyland was brilliant. I remember us kids being so knackered that we fell asleep on the floor waiting for Tinkerbell to fly out of the castle at midnight. Mum had to wake us up just in time to see Tinkerbell whizzing through the air for what can't have been more than two seconds!

Our first holiday together in Mexico. Before I nearly drowned…

Beach babe

Wayne would love to go to Disneyland in Florida but I've told him how tiring it is, and once he finishes the football season all he wants to do is relax. It's harder for Wayne to switch off than for me. People recognize him wherever he goes and come up asking for autographs. Sometimes that's nice and we have a laugh, though at other times we wish we could get away from it all.

We've been to some great places over the past few years – La Manga and Sardinia on England training camps, and trips to New York, Paris, Barcelona and Madrid. In terms of relaxation the best places have been Barbados, Dubai and our boating holiday around the south of France.

Barbados 2004 and a romantic meal for two on the beach.

Wayne would go to Barbados every year if he could. It is beautiful, the people are lovely, and the luxury hotel we stay in, the Sandy Lane, is right by the sea and near miles of white sandy beaches. We'll go jet-skiing, water-skiing, snorkelling, swimming with the turtles, or we'll take a ride over the island in a helicopter, or maybe have a treatment at the spa – it's totally relaxing and you can't do anything but enjoy yourself. Just talking about it makes me want to go there! The second time we stayed for a few days then flew out to meet up with my two brothers in Jamaica, with the intention of staying there for the rest of the holiday. But I didn't like Jamaica as much. I didn't like the complex and I got bitten to death by mosquitos, so after a couple of days we flew back to Barbados.

In Dubai we usually stay at a resort called Jumeirah, with all different hotels. In the past we have stayed in one of the Beachcomber villas and it's really chilled out. You get taken to your section of the beach in little buggies and they will bring you back at the end of the day. The resort has about forty different restaurants and shops, but most of the time we just take it easy, lie on the beach, and read the odd book. We're not big readers but holidays give you more time for books. The last time around I read *Fashion Babylon*, a gossipy read about the industry. It's good. I try to eat healthily when we're away, but you know what it's like when you're on holiday. We will do loads of swimming and maybe a few sit-ups, then towards the end of the holiday Wayne will start going to the gym, because he knows as soon as he returns home he's straight into training.

I went back to Dubai with just my mates and we stayed at the only seven-star hotel in the world, the Burj Al Arab.

What makes a seven-star hotel? That's what I wondered. But when you see the suites you understand where the extra two stars come from. They are basically luxury flats, decorated in deep reds, purples and golds, with a living area and kitchen downstairs and a spiral staircase that leads up to the bedrooms. The staff can't do enough for you. It's incredible. The whole resort was great for me and the girls, because there are these shopping malls, such as Emirates Towers, that have everything: Harvey Nichols, Topshop, Debenhams … all of them! Then there are great restaurants and bars, and in the hotel itself there's a bar that seems to be miles up in the sky and looks out over the whole city. Me and Wayne went back there when we had an unexpected week off because he was banned from playing, and after we'd been around the south of France, which was the best holiday I've ever been on.

I can't wait for our next holiday together. I wouldn't mind a few days in Las Vegas but I'm not that desperate. I'd probably prefer to try Los Angeles, simply because you read so much about Hollywood and everything, so it would be good to see what it's like for myself. Wayne's always fancied Australia as well, but because of the jetlag I think you need to spend three or four weeks over there, so maybe that will be somewhere to go when Wayne's retired from football. If it's down to me then the next time we go away I'd love it to be to Mauritius. Or, if we got a boat, it would be brilliant to sail around the Italian coast. Whatever we decide, I'm sure we'll have a great time.

Hot stuff

The sun's shining down, the sky's blue and there's sand between your toes. Complete the perfect summer look by making sure your beach bag contains the following:

A wide-brimmed straw hat

Bought from the local market. The more battered the better for that shabby-chic effect.

Long and short kaftans

Very Moroccan, very now. Can be worn on the beach, to dinner and for partying.

At least one well-cut bikini

Skimpy is good as long as you're not falling out!

Over-sized sunglasses

For 1970s glam.

High flip-flops/sandals

Look to the local supermarket for cheap and original designs.

A cotton sarong

The most versatile piece of cloth known to fashion. Can be tied round the neck and belted to make a dress, folded and wrapped for a shirt skirt, or worn over the shoulders to protect you from the sun.

chapter twenty

give it a go: that's my attitude to life

There are newspapers who say my earnings in the past year or so have amounted to somewhere in the region of £5 million to £6 million. All I can say to those kinds of figures is, 'I wish!' I couldn't actually tell you how much I'm really worth. Through contracts, endorsements like Asda and my column in *Closer*, I know I've been fortunate to have earned quite a lot of money over the last couple of years or so, but that side of our affairs is entrusted to our management company.

Believe it or not, no amount of money will change me as a person. One of the weirdest and often annoying things about being in the spotlight is having other people comment on your life and personality. In the beginning, after I'd just met Wayne, the newspapers had me down as some kind of gold-digger. Nowadays, because I have my own income, all of a sudden journalists paint me in a more positive light – as though everything's okay now because I'm spending my earnings and not Wayne's. It just goes to show that while money doesn't necessarily change you, it can change other people's opinions about you.

My relationship with Wayne has never been about money, and that hasn't altered over the years. Neither has having my own career and the income that goes with it turned me into some kind of Ms Independent Woman. I've never had the view that a girl needs to go out and get a career in order to somehow justify her existence. If you are in a couple and you've no need to work, and your partner's happy to support you, then I don't think there's anything wrong with that. My mum stopped working early in her marriage to bring up me and my brothers and my dad was happy with that arrangement. My mum and dad have never had separate bank accounts and all the money that came into the house was shared. That's always been the same with me and Wayne. We have our own accounts, but also a joint account for the household bills and furnishings. People should have the choice of how they want to organize their lives and not be dictated to by what's supposedly right or wrong.

If a woman wants to go to work or stay at home, then whatever works for her relationship is what matters.

For a long while after I first met Wayne I was criticized for not having a career of my own, but I was young and the intention was always to start doing things once the right opportunities came along, rather than jump at any old offer. I'm glad we made that decision because now I'm really happy about the way my career is progressing.

One of the real positives out of all of this is being able to help my family financially. Not that they need help, but they've looked after me throughout my life and so it's nice to be able to give them something back. It was a lovely feeling to buy them a new house. It's great to be able to do things like that with your own money. Just as it was fantastic to be able to go out and buy Wayne an Aston Martin for his twenty-first birthday. For me, earning money is more about what it allows you to do for other people rather than yourself.

I would probably point to the *Vogue* shoot in 2005 as the time when my career took off in a big way. Before then I had done shoots for the *Sunday Mirror* and the *Mail*'s *Night and Day* magazine, but nothing in the way of commercial deals. That really all started with Asda. I'd done bits and bobs before, but nothing like the Asda deal, which was worth more than a million pounds.

I had been approached by another high-street store when Asda came in with a better offer and a contract to be the face of their Must-Have range. The fashion aspect appealed to me and the fact I'd been brought up shopping at that supermarket. Initially the contract was a joint deal which meant working with Wayne, but due to his pre-World Cup injury, Wayne had to pull out of all commercial deals to concentrate on getting fit. Fortunately my business manager Paul was able to secure a deal involving me on my own. I understand there's some cynical people out there who don't believe I actually wear the clothes, but I do. They do some great pieces and I can't resist a bargain. I'm not saying I wear everything or that the whole range suits me, but the same can be said of my favourite high-fashion labels like Chloé and Stella McCartney. The other week I was wearing a grey jumper-dress from Asda and a couple of people asked me where it was from. I could tell by their faces they weren't expecting me to say Asda, which is a great compliment to their designs.

The George at Asda advert was shot in Portugal and it was also really special. I had my mates ringing me up telling me they'd been sat in front of the telly, watching the adverts all night, waiting for me to come on! At one of mum's girly nights, all my aunties and cousins started singing *Pretty Woman* at mo, until I told them all to shut up! Inside I was really proud.

When I launched the Must-Have range in May 2006 wearing a £10 khaki shirt dress, over 45,000 were sold just hours after going in store.

The Asda contract lasts for eighteen months and there is talk of me designing a clothes range for them. That isn't finalized yet, but it is something I'd be really interested in doing. I really enjoy the work with Asda and George, and I think Paul is going to talk about an extension to the contract with them.

I'm really hoping we can work something out along those lines because the George at Asda range is a really exciting brand to be working with. I didn't know until I began working with them but apparently in the UK one in ten pieces of clothing worn has the George at Asda label. That's amazing when you think about it. It's also really flattering to think you personally have an effect on what people are wearing. When I launched the Must-Have range in May 2006 wearing a £10 khaki shirt dress, over 45,000 were sold just hours after going in store. They told me it was one of George's fastest-selling items in the label's sixteen-year history.

The cropped shorts I wore sold 70,000 pairs and the really top-value £3 racer-back vest sold more than 100,000.

When you're talking about finding fashion bargains on the high street, you've really got to include the effect and influence Asda and others have on people's style. It's a relatively new fashion phenomenon that's only going to get bigger and bigger. That's why it's something that's great to be a part of.

Looking back, it's mad to think how my working life has turned out. From the start I was criticized by the newspapers, questioning me, asking why I was famous. What had I done to deserve any of this? was the general opinion. For the record, I've never regarded myself as a celebrity and I never will. I'd go so far as to say I'm well-known. I'm not an actress or a pop star or a model, even though I promote clothes. Hopefully, through my fashion and the way I go about life, I am simply someone other girls relate to, and that's why I'm doing what I do now.

One of the most rewarding parts of my career at the moment is writing my column for *Closer*. The magazine has a readership of around 500,000 a week, and not only does it give me the opportunity to right some of the wrongs that have been written about me in the press, but it's also allowed me to pursue my interest in journalism, which started back at school with media studies.

Each Monday, the editor will call and we'll discuss what's going to go in that week's issue. Generally, it's quite a girly column, with my views on fashion and lifestyle and what I've been up to for the previous few days. I get great feedback from readers through letters and emails, with queries ranging from what colour shoes they should be wearing to what outfit to buy for a wedding. You soon appreciate there's quite a responsibility that comes with the job and people do take the things you say very seriously. One time I wrote that waistcoats were out of style, and that week I was spotted in my local supermarket wearing one. 'Excuse me!' said this reader. 'I thought you said waistcoats were out?' I had to explain that they weren't so much out as not as popular any more!

Wayne reads my column every week, but I think that's just to check up on what I'm writing about him. Every now and again, say when I've said something about how he likes my curves,

Taking the family for a spin at Eurodisney.

for instance, he'll have a moan asking why I've written about this or that. I know he doesn't mind really. I've recently signed a new deal with the magazine, so I'm sure he'll feature in a few more columns to come.

All the offers of work and magazine requests that we receive go through my manager Paul and my publicist Ian Monk. If I accepted everything that came my way then I could probably fill my diary twice over. From the very start, though, since Paul began looking after my career, we decided to be choosy about what I'll say yes to. It's all too easy in this business to think about your bank balance rather than taking a long-term strategy. In terms of endorsements like Asda, the deal I had with LG Chocolate mobile phones or the advert me and Wayne did for Coca Cola, it's important to go with a product that you not only believe in but one that sits comfortably with your character and image. For instance, my work with George at Asda allows me to promote fashion, which I am passionate about. You wouldn't believe the amount of strange offers I get, or what my name's associated with. Ian Monk sorts through the majority of these kinds of approaches and discusses the merits of them with both Paul and Ian before I see them, turning down those they know I'm not going to like. But I like to see most of the proposals before they are rejected.

One of the ideas I did turn down first of all, only to change my mind at a later date, was making my own fitness DVD. I think it's the unwritten rule of entering the public eye that every female has to make a fitness video! I initially said no, because it didn't seem to be me and I wasn't simply going to make one because that's what everyone else did. By the time I was approached again by Universal, I had actually started to go to the gym, I'd lost a bit of puppy fat and toned up. I can't deny the money was good, but I really enjoyed putting *Coleen McLoughlin's Brand New Body Workout* together.

At first I was a bit apprehensive because the producer was asking me to lead a group of girls through the routines and I had to tell them I wasn't a fitness instructor! Then we got a proper fitness instructor in – Elise Lindsay, who's still my personal trainer today – and I co-presented.

I worked very hard with Elise in the eight weeks before we started shooting the DVD, getting into shape. We filmed over two days and I was expecting there to be loads and loads of takes and that everything would be edited together at the end. That's not how it works at all. You run through the routine, then you might have to do it again because someone's laces were undone or you were out of sync with the other girls. Basically, you keep on going until you get it right. I was knackered by the end of it!

The DVD did well, but it was competing with so many others. I think Charlie Brooks, who used to be in *EastEnders*, beat me to number one in the bestsellers list, but I'm still proud of it. I think you need to lose a lot of weight to have a really big seller, whereas I only lost a few pounds and toned up. Both Davina and Jordan did theirs post-pregnancy and so you see the difference and think, 'That is incredible!' Maybe post-pregnancy fitness DVDs are the way to go next time … although I might wait a little while yet!

Television is one of the areas I'm really interested in. A while ago I was asked to go on that celebrity equestrian competition. For some reason people think I'm really into horses, but I don't ride as often as I'd like. I want to go riding more, but I don't think I'm ready for show jumping yet.

Not all my career moves are motivated by financial gain. Sometimes it's a case of going with an idea because it's good for my profile and image. That was the case when Channel Five approached me to make a programme about my life. We'd had similar approaches before, but the timing had never been right or we knew the makers were angling for a different story. With *Coleen's Secrets* in 2005 we had a certain degree of editorial control, and it gave the public an opportunity to see the real me, as opposed to all the negative press that seemed to surround me at the time. I didn't want it to be a biographical documentary, just because I was so young, so in the end it focused on my love of fashion, with bits about my life, and the producers gave it the twist of me having to choose the perfect dress for an awards do, which turned out to be the National Television Awards. To be honest, it was meant to be the Fashion Rocks awards but we couldn't finish everything in time! The programme went out and it had a really good response.

All of a sudden, people were more positive about me, so it was good for the public to see that I wasn't the shopaholic footballer's girlfriend the newspapers had been talking about for so long.

The one thing I remember about that documentary was going to the National Television Awards after-show party wearing nearly £1 million worth of jewellery that had been loaned to me by Chopard. The documentary was over by then, and so the crew and I had a few drinks and danced all night. I didn't think about it at the time, but at the end of the night I sadly handed over the earrings to

the security men. I was just thankful they were still in one piece.

Doing the *Tonight* show with Sir Trevor McDonald was another step in a different direction, as well as building on the experience I'd gained from the Channel Five documentary. The main attraction was that it was not about me but about a serious subject that, given my sister Rosie's condition, I felt strongly about: caring for disabled children and talking about the lack of funding in children's hospices. They asked me if I'd like to present the show, and although I felt nervous I felt it was something I should do. It wasn't that I was worried about being in front of the camera, it was just that it was going to be me asking questions, being the journalist.

I'm quite shy when I meet new people – maybe not shy exactly, but I'm quiet until I get to know them. That's why I always loved acting at school, because once you were up on stage you weren't yourself any more. But I went to lunch with Sir Trevor and he told me to be myself and to ask the questions that I wanted answered. He was great and I'm so glad I went ahead with the programme. What became known as 'Coleen's Campaign' is one of my proudest achievements.

Although I've first-hand experience of the problems involved with caring for children like Rosie, researching for the *Tonight* show really opened my eyes to how desperate the situation was and still is for others. And the more I learned the more I wanted to do something to help.

There are more than twenty thousand children in England currently suffering with either life-threatening or life-limiting conditions. They require twenty-four-hour care which puts an incredible emotional, physical and mental strain on the rest of the family.

Hospices like Claire House on the Wirral, where our Rosie goes every now and again, provide nursing, accommodation and amazing state-of-the-art facilities which essentially allow those families a break from the pressures they face day after day. Claire House, for instance, has six rooms for children and five rooms for families to stay, plus a new wing which has four bedrooms for disabled teenagers. It's a great place. People often think of a hospice as somewhere you go to die but they're not at all. They're full of fun and laughter and love all around.

In England there are 34 hospices like Claire House but I discovered that only one fifth of the children who could benefit from their facilities actually have access to them. The trouble is these hospices are extremely expensive to run – on average they need £2 million a year just to keep going. What shocked me is that the government provides only 5 per cent of that money and the rest of the funding comes through charitable donations. I couldn't believe it. I couldn't understand how so many of the hospices which were doing something so brilliant and necessary were in danger of closure due to lack of government support. I wanted to highlight the issue and get the government to do something.

The feedback I received from that programme was unbelievable. The day after it went out I was in a supermarket and I must have had six people come up to me saying how brilliant the show had been. We'd all watched it together at my mum's house and everyone had been crying because it was quite sad at times. Afterwards, my phone must have gone off about fifty times. The next thing we knew, my mum had people knocking at her door saying they wanted to donate money to our local children's hospice, Claire House, which was featured. There was even a local artist who asked if he could paint a children's mural on the hospice walls. There were loads of really lovely gestures like that.

Later on in 2006 I did a follow-up programme with Sir Trevor. Not only had the first show raised the general public's awareness of the problems facing children's hospices but the government had also sat up and taken notice. As a result of our campaign and the documentary Tony Blair had agreed to a review of the long-term funding of children's hospices in England and promised to provide £27 million over the next three years to go towards their running costs.

That was great news and we were all pleased that at last something was being done. But when you consider that £27m spread over three years only amounts to 10 per cent of the funding each hospice actually needs, then you realize there's still a lot of work and campaigning to be done. I care passionately about this and I for one won't let up until children's hospices receive the fair and adequate funding they so deserve.

I don't think I'm alone in saying the hardest aspect of being a so-called name in the spotlight is being asked to do charity work and having to turn it down.

I hate that, but I get so many requests from charities and good causes that I've had to put a limit on what I do. I even have people posting letters through my door asking for help, and although I'd like to say yes to everyone, realistically I know that's not possible.

Most of the work and funding I do centres around a few charities and causes that I had connections with before I made the newspapers, such as Alder Hey Children's Hospital in Liverpool, Claire House Children's Hospice, where Rosie goes, as well as some work for Kids Connect, a children's charity for Rett syndrome sufferers, which my mum and dad also work with. I'm also linked to the Breast Cancer Fund through my work with Asda. Both me and Wayne try to focus on a few specific causes and do the best we can for them.

My career has really taken off in the last couple of years, including writing this book. I always had hopes but I could never have imagined it would turn out the way it has, and that I'd be fortunate enough to earn the kind of money I am now. There was and never has been a grand plan, but I've always been open to ideas and having a go at new things. And Wayne has supported me throughout. If anything, my career and having to deal with the media on a regular basis have brought us closer together. It means he doesn't have to worry about me sitting at home with nothing to do while he's off playing for Man United, and we've been able to share our experiences and learn from them.

Would Wayne ever have a problem if I was earning more money than him? I don't think that's likely to happen, but the answer would be no. He's not like that. Wayne is a person who's happy for other people when they're doing well, he doesn't get jealous because someone has got more than him.

Would the two of us be happy together if we didn't have the money we have now? Yes. That's all I can say. Both of us come from the same backgrounds and we wouldn't know or be any different if we'd never had the money we do have. I know people who have nothing and they are completely happy with themselves. Me and Wayne would be exactly the same.

chapter twenty-one

my whole life ahead of me

The last few years have been so unbelievable that it's hard to know what lies ahead. There's a part of me that's still the six-teen-year-old girl who made that joke in the 2002 St John Bosco High School yearbook about how in ten years' time she wanted to be famous and living a life of luxury, but so much has changed in my life since I wrote those words. If you had asked me then to imagine what the last few years were going to bring, then there's no way I could have predicted all that has happened. How could I predict my relationship with Wayne, how I was suddenly caught up in this whirlwind of press and attention, or the rollercoaster of emotions that comes from being in the spotlight and having our private lives scrutinized on a daily basis? How could I have imagined all the amazing work opportunities I've been lucky enough to receive, from fashion shoots for *Vogue* to TV documentaries with Sir Trevor McDonald and becoming the face of a massive advertising campaign for a brand as big as George at Asda? Nobody thinks all those things are going to happen to them.

Given all that's gone on in the past, it's hard to know what's going to happen in the future. I know I want to be married and have children with Wayne, I can tell you that much. But as far as my career goes, it's difficult to know exactly how things will work out.

Five years ago I thought I was probably going to go to university and study Performing Arts or Journalism, but then there was the broken bicycle and a kiss in the local churchyard, and everything changed for ever.

I have a few ideas of what I'd like to be doing workwise. I'd love to continue my column with *Closer*, to still be working with Asda, maybe designing my own range of clothes. Ideally, it would be great to gain more experience in television. That's an area I've really enjoyed in the past and I think I've learned from the programmes I've appeared on. My publicist and manager receive requests all the time, but it's a matter of choosing the right road to take. There have been approaches made in the past that I've turned down because I just didn't feel ready. A lot of those involved 'live' TV – such as *GMTV* asking me to report from London Fashion Week, or being invited to appear on the *Loose Women* panel – both of which I didn't feel confident enough to take on at the time. Today I feel I can handle that kind of challenge a whole lot better. People have always said I'd be good at presenting, so maybe it's time I believed them. Until I try it, I won't know if I'm good enough. And that's always been my philosophy, to have a go and see what happens. I'm not scared of doing that.

Who knows if people, the newspapers and the magazines will

still be interested in me in a year's time or further into the future? I'm more than aware of how and why I've been fortunate enough for companies to want me to endorse their business, and why I receive the coverage I do. I'm seen as the girl-next-door, one that every other girl can relate to. That's the marketing speak, at least. As far as I'm concerned, I'm just being me. But I'm also aware that people in this business sometimes only have a certain period of time in the spotlight. Who knows how long my time's going to last before someone else comes along? Growing older means I won't be able to go on being the young girl-next-door forever. People might not be so interested in Coleen, the woman-next-door! I don't know. I hope that certain work, like Asda and *Closer*, will continue, but you never know.

Of course, I have my dreams. I look at someone like Cat Deeley and admire what she's done with her career. She appears to be very nice and has always seemed to make the right choices with her career, working on a wide range of shows and growing with them. If I did decide to try to be a TV presenter, I'd love to be able to talk to her and people like Ant and Dec about the job because they make it look so effortless, which I understand it's not.

I've always said that if things don't work out or I become unhappy, I will go back to my studies and try for drama school, or at least do classes. I've never lost that love for performing. I see so many shows and the thought of acting still excites me.

What I do know is that I've never taken for granted where I am now. As you know, I hate the word fame, because I just don't see myself as famous. Over time, I've become used to walking into the newsagent's and seeing myself on the covers of magazines, but that doesn't mean I am any less excited. I still go, 'I can't quite get a grip on it, that's me up there! And I'm on the cover and people are buying that!' Whether that's going to be a part of my life forever, I don't know. If it all went tomorrow, there are parts of it I would miss. But I wouldn't let it get me down. I'd just get on with my life.

I'm just taking life as it comes. I can't say I'm planning on world domination and being a superstar in however many years' time.

I'm not an actress who can say they'd like to win an Oscar by the time they're fifty, or a pop star who wants so many best-selling records. My career can still go in so many directions, and all I want to do is build on what I've done already. I try to take each day as it comes: if it happens, it happens, and if it doesn't, it doesn't.

It's hard to know what the years ahead are going to bring, but I still think about the future. Other people talk about being a footballer's wife and all the glamour that goes with it, but there are no guarantees in the game and sometimes you don't know what's around the corner. I'm sure Wayne would love to spend the rest of his career at Manchester United, but we don't know what's in store, whether we might have to move abroad at some stage or whatever. I always see myself staying in this country because I'm quite a hometown girl and I like being around my friends and family. However, you never know what the years might bring. I wouldn't like to move now, but maybe that's because I'm still young.

The reality of being a footballer is that it's a short career. Every now and again I'll ask Wayne what he's going to be doing after he's finished playing. That might seem a long time away, but you do have to think that in fourteen or fifteen years' time his career will probably be over. You see players retiring all the time, like Wayne's friend Duncan Ferguson, and it's hard for them to stop playing the game they love. I think Wayne will feel the same way and he'll just want to keep playing and playing. Unfortunately, the only way you can prolong your career is to drop down the divisions, and if you've played at the top all your life you want to finish at the top. It's very difficult just to call it a day. Maybe Wayne will keep involved in football by going into management or coaching. What would that make me? A football manager's wife!

Now and again, I have times when I imagine what our wedding's going to be like. I know I want it to be a big, traditional wedding, but that's as far as it goes.

That's all for another day. What we can plan for is the day we're going to get married and have children. That kind of planning isn't difficult, because we love each other and that's what both of us want to happen.

Wayne would love to have a child right now, but I think I'm too young at the moment. It's been said in some interviews that I want to get married before I have kids, but that's not the case. It's not that I'm set on being married before we have children, it's just that I'd prefer it to be that way round. If I fell pregnant then I would be made up, but I'm not at the stage in my life where I want to be pregnant. I just feel like I've got a lot to do with my life before I start a family. And Wayne is just at the beginning of his career too, a job that takes him away a lot of the time, so at the moment, with the way our lives are, it's hard enough to find time together to have a peaceful day to ourselves without adding the responsibilities of a family.

Of course, having children is a big topic among all my mates. We talk about pregnancy and what we'd do if we became pregnant now. I've always said I'd be happy, but I'm fortunate enough to be in a financial situation where I could cope with having a family. If you think about it, most people plan having children around whether they feel emotionally ready and comfortable enough to afford caring for a child and their essential needs.

Me and Wayne would like to get married in the near future and then we can think about having children. We have talked about what year we reckon would be best, but, like everything, we have got to plan it around the football calendar. If we want a honeymoon then we will need to get married in the summer, and that's still got to be a year when there are no Euros or World Cups to give ourselves enough time.

Now and again, I have times when I imagine what our wedding's going to be like. I know I want it to be a big, traditional wedding, but that's as far as it goes. I haven't got a clue what kind of dress I want to wear or any of those details. And anyway, I would change my mind from month to month! We have ideas of what we would like, but when the time comes we're going to get a wedding planner to help us put everything together.

Right now, I don't know when the wedding's going to be or where it's going to be. There were stories in the newspapers of how we were going to be married in a local church in Croxteth, Queen of Martyrs, as it's right by mine and Wayne's old family homes, but that's just the press talking. Although it would be nice to go back to my old church, St Teresa's, to get married, the church stands on a main road, and for security reasons I just don't think it would be realistic.

Whether I like it or not, my private life isn't private any more, and it's hard to make these kinds of decisions without thinking you're going to upset someone.

In the past I have been inundated with offers about doing a deal with a magazine like *OK!* or *Hello!* and selling the exclusive to our wedding, but at the moment I really don't know how I feel about that. It's not necessarily about the money, but I've spoken to other people and they've said how hard it is for everything to go smoothly unless you come to some kind of agreement before-hand. The last thing you want at your wedding is photographers everywhere ruining the day and trying to get a picture. At least when you do a deal with a magazine, they organize all the security and make sure no one else gets in.

Having said that, I wouldn't want anyone controlling my day. My main concern is that I would want all our guests, including any celebrities, to enjoy themselves. That's why we haven't decided whether to go with a magazine or not.

Whether I like it or not, my private life isn't private any more, and it's hard to make these kinds of decisions without thinking you're going to upset someone. We've got to accept that we are in the public eye and it's not going to be a normal wedding. However, my wish is to make it as normal and traditional as possible. If that means working with a magazine then that's what I'll do. Our wedding should be about me and Wayne, our families and our friends, and we shouldn't be worrying about pictures being in the newspapers the next day.

So that's my world so far. Maybe it's just how you imagined it, or maybe it has thrown up a few surprises. I'm not very old but sometimes it feels like me and Wayne have been through so much. And, if I'm truthful, I wouldn't change anything. I enjoy the good times and learn from the bad. That's life. I once did an interview for *Marie Claire* magazine and they asked me how I liked to be seen by people. 'I want to come across as myself,' I said. 'For who I am. For going out and having a go.' I still stick by that. Nothing's changed.

If you put a yearbook in front of me now and asked me to write down where I wanted to be in ten years' time, then I know exactly what my entry would be. To be happy and healthy, married to Wayne, with a family of our own. That's all. Nothing else matters in the end.

'... fast-forward 12 months and they say I'm the new Cilla Black!'

I've just re-read that last paragraph and it made me think how fast the months have flown by since those words were written, and how things have changed – especially career-wise. Little did I know this time last year I'd be a best-selling author, have my own perfume on the shelves of Selfridges and be talked about in the newspapers as the new Cilla Black.

Believe me, when I first started work on *Welcome to My World* I hadn't a clue how well it was going to do. I never imagined the hardback edition would sell more than 100,000 copies and the former editor of the *Mirror*, Piers Morgan, would be complaining that my book was keeping his autobiography off the top of the bestsellers' list! To write a bestseller was beyond my wildest dreams.

As I've said before, there's never been a master plan. My philosophy has always been the same – if it feels right, then give it a go and see what happens. And things do always seem to happen to me.

Back in August, the success of the book resulted in me launching my own signature fragrance, 'Coleen x'. I'd never thought about bringing my own perfume out before Paul, our manager, was contacted by one of the big perfume and beauty manufacturing companies, Fragrance and Beauty. In the beginning, I was a bit wary of people thinking, 'Oh, Coleen's just jumping on the bandwagon', probably in the same way I'd worried about the reaction to my fitness DVD. But then FAB put forward this ten-year-deal, where I'd not only be bringing out my own perfume but there was also the chance to create my own range of beauty and make-up products. I just thought, 'Fantastic! How lucky am I?'

At the start, I wasn't sure how much input I would have, but I ended up travelling down to Grasse, in the south of France, where the world-famous Robertet perfumery laboratories are based. A few days before I went to France I did a questionnaire that the perfumery had sent me about what kind of scent I wanted to create, what smells I liked and what my favourite perfumes were. So when we got to the laboratories, they had already analysed my questionnaire and had prepared fourteen fragrances based on my answers. I was shown around the laboratories and saw how the perfumes are created, and the way the petals and everything are crushed down to create the liquid that the fragrance will be made from. Eventually, we narrowed the selection to four choices and I went home to Liverpool to test them on my mum, friends and family. There was no competition, everyone went for the same one – a citrusy smell with a hint of amber and sweet orange.

Launching my perfume at Selfridges.

My mum and my nan, me, my cousins, my aunties and friends … we all smell the same now! You think I'm joking, don't you? No, really, as ever, everyone's been really supportive and it's lovely to have them help me make the final decision.

On the one hand, it's really exciting for a girl to have her own perfume out there on the shelves. Even more so when I learnt that Selfridges, who have never stocked a celebrity perfume brand before, not even Jennifer Lopez, chose to make mine exclusive to their stores before the national launch. I was so made up by that. But that doesn't make it any less weird to have a perfume out there with your name on it. My mum said she went to Selfridges in the Trafford Centre in Manchester and she overheard girls going up to the beauty counter asking for some 'Coleen, please'. That was odd for her, people asking for a bottle of her daughter! You never think of that when you're buying other people's perfumes. Yeah, mum's right, it's weird, but a nice weird.

I never really wanted to be a model or believed that I could be in adverts and then I ended up working with George at Asda.

The other big change to my life in the work sense is the two-year deal I signed with ITV. The first episode of my programme comes out on ITV2 not long after the Christmas holiday season so it might well be already on television by the time you read this.

After I did the Trevor McDonald show we had loads of offers but I didn't want to do just anything and, if I'm being honest, I was terrified of doing TV. I just didn't feel as if I had enough experience.

We'd turned down a lot of approaches, then Endemol – the people behind *Big Brother* – came up with this pitch called *Coleen's Real Women*. The idea is to get real-sized women like me of all ages into advertising campaigns. It's an eight-part series, and each show sees me and a camera running around the streets of London, Liverpool, Manchester, Bristol and Birmingham ...

Filming my new TV series, *Coleen's Real Women*.

everywhere, searching for new, real, modelling talent. We invite everyone, maybe as many as 120 girls, to a casting day. That's whittled down to ten, then our final three eventually go forward for modelling jobs at the likes of Pretty Polly, Sweaty Betty and Avon.

The whole concept appealed because that's exactly what happened to me. I never really wanted to be a model or believed that I could be in adverts and then I ended up working with George at Asda.

The first day, running up to a girl standing in Carnaby Street buying a sandwich at lunch, I felt dead nervous, but the more times I did it the more confident I got. There were rumours in the newspapers that I was going to be given my own chat show, but I don't feel ready for that. *Coleen's Real Women* is me being more my natural self so it doesn't feel that stressful. The most horrible bit is on the casting days when the girls turn up and at the end of the morning we have to tell them they've not made it through to the next stage. I'm no Simon Cowell, even though I love watching him, and the first time I hated it. I said: 'Can't someone else get up and read the names out?' but they were like, 'No, you've got to do it.' That was the worst part. That and being away from Wayne and home so much during the filming.

I've signed up for two years with ITV with the idea that I'll do *Coleen's Real Women*, then I might pop up on one or two other shows and, next year, hopefully do another bigger show. The intention is to start off slowly and see where it leads. So, not quite the new Cilla Black, as some newspapers have labelled me, but, then again, I'm happy with being known simply as Coleen.

'The best days of our lives and the best night of my life'

Last March the hardback edition of this book went on sale and I have to say things went crazy. Crazy in a great way but it feels like I haven't stopped since (okay, apart from a little holiday or two in the likes of the Côte d'Azur and Las Vegas – after all, every girl needs time out to relax and recharge!). One minute I was worrying whether anyone would be interested enough to buy a book about me, the next I knew I was going on *GMTV* and *T4*, touring the country doing signings, then launching my fragrance and TV

At my book launch at Cricket.

career. In between, I had my twenty-first birthday and began organizing our wedding for this summer. Wayne was pretty busy too, winning his first Premiership medal with Manchester United, and then getting back into pre-season training. Then there was the unfortunate injury to his foot on the opening day of the season. Other than Wayne's injuries, it's been a brilliant twelve months for both of us.

The book signing tour ended up being amazing. I say ended up because at the start I just didn't want to do it. I'm not a pop star or an actress, and I didn't believe people would turn up – I was dreading the thought of me sitting there in an empty bookshop with a pile of books beside me.

My final book signing with my management team: Jane my PA, Steve, security and Paul my manager.

I'd been on *GMTV* with Fiona Phillips and Ben Shephard doing my first live television interview and that in itself had been a nerve-wracking experience, but they both made me feel at ease. Then I went and recorded an interview with Steve Jones for *T4*. He brought up the fact I'd had a walk-on part in *Hollyoaks*, and I was thinking, 'Oh no, they're going to show it!' It turned out they had been searching for the clip but, luckily, they couldn't find it.

The actual book launch itself was held at my favourite shop, Cricket in Liverpool. Where else? That was a great night. Me, Justine the owner and Lorraine the stylist came up with this idea of taking a trip down memory lane and the store was full of mannequins wearing some of my favourite dresses that are featured in this book. We even had one done up in my old school uniform – not the original, I might add. It was a really lovely night, full of family and friends, made even more special when I learned that *Welcome to My World* was going to be number one in the book charts.

But the success of the TV appearances and the launch didn't stop me fretting about the book signings. I remember being on my way to one of the first ones in Liverpool and asking my friend to go and check if anyone had turned up. She called me and went: 'Erm, there's quite a few and some have been queueing for hours.' She wasn't joking. When I turned up there seemed to be hundreds of people there. I couldn't believe it. And it was the same wherever I went – Leeds, Newcastle, Manchester, even London – up and down the country. As you can imagine, at Waterstones in Bold Street, Liverpool all my family and friends came along – so many that my granddad couldn't get in. He started queueing but security weren't allowing any more people through the doors so he went home. My dad was like, 'Why were you waiting outside? Why didn't you ring us!' In the end he got a taxi back to town and we got him in! Two of my cousins weren't so lucky. Security had to keep turning people away because apparently there were quite a few people pretending to be my cousins that day, but I saw them at the end!

I know I was worried in the beginning but I loved every minute of that two-week tour and am really grateful to everyone who came along. At times it was overwhelming, for me and others. I remember this one girl in Newcastle who was hyperventilating so much she had to be helped into a chair so she could calm down!

It was great meeting everyone, young and old, girls and lads who said they were there for their girlfriends (but I wasn't quite sure!); all those fellow lovers of shopping who asked me to write 'Keep on Shopping' in their books! It was unforgettable.

I suppose one of the reasons why I was so stressed at the start was because the promotional tour coincided with me organizing my twenty-first birthday party. The intention always was to have a big, big party and celebrate the day with all my family and friends. But the speculation in the magazines and newspapers had me having the celebrity bash of the year, with a guest list, or so they reckoned, reading like a Hollywood film premiere. It came to the point where I had friends ringing up asking who was going to be there and I had to tell them not to get too excited because I was only inviting the people I wanted, i.e. friends and family. Yeah, there might be a few footballers there like Wayne's mates Rio and Steven Gerrard, but that's because of his job; celebrity-wise we don't really have that many friends like that.

And although Paul had organized a deal with *Hello!*, that was as much about security as anything else, as I've said here before. I was determined it wasn't going to turn into a celebrity party. When Wayne had his eighteenth there'd been a similar deal. It was a fantastic night but Wayne wasn't interested in organizing it and all these actors from *EastEnders* and other soaps were invited by the magazine. Even Busted turned up! Wayne looks back on it now and we have a laugh. 'I can't believe it,' he'll say. 'I don't have a clue who half the people were at my birthday party!'

Still, no matter what I said, the newspapers had a field day with rumours about who was going to be there and whatnot. They even said I'd issued all guests with a book of rules telling them how to behave and everything. I hadn't at all. The invites were designed to be stood up with pages that flipped over like a calendar. On the back page all it said was that cameras weren't allowed and I asked everyone to please respect all the guests, just because I didn't want all Wayne's football mates being asked for autographs all night. I was gutted when the press made it into something it wasn't. One particular newspaper was especially vindictive, but they were made to apologize in the end and pay damages which were donated to one of the charities I support.

On the day itself none of that mattered. The party was held in the grounds of Thornton Manor, just over the water from Liverpool in Merseyside. I wanted an elegant circus theme. That was my big idea. There were three marquees all joined – a reception area, a lounge and then the main party room. All were decked out in white and lilac and silver. Outside was my very own mini-fun-fair, complete with side-stalls, waltzers and a Miami high flyer ride. Inside, the guests – there were around 300 in total – were

greeted by stilt-walkers, acrobats and trapeze artists swinging off the ceiling. It was brilliant. There was an ice bar with my name carved into it. That was funny because everyone kept putting their drinks down on it and they kept sliding off! The party planners had decorated the spaces with large, gilt-framed photographs of my work from the likes of *Vogue* and *Marie Claire*, and there was another one full of pictures of all my friends and family. My mum and dad, nan and granddad, cousins, everyone … that was dead good. In the reception tent there was a singer doing Lionel Richie kind of numbers, the cast of Rat Pack were in the lounge area and the Beat Freaks were in the main party room. I didn't want a sit-down dinner, so there were food stations in the lounge, each one serving different foods from around the world. It was a dream party and I made sure I was going to enjoy it.

There was an ice bar with my name carved into it. That was funny because everyone kept putting their drinks down on it and they kept sliding off!

I'd chosen to wear a Grecian-style Amanda Wakeley gown that I found in Harvey Nichols. I tried it on and instantly fell in love with it. When I arrived home and showed my mum she said, 'Yeah, that's the one.' Jacob, the jeweller from New York, sent me over these bangles for the night and earrings which I later learnt were worth around £250,000! They looked amazing. And Wayne bought me a new ring. I'd always wanted a yellow diamond ring and he bought me this 12.07 carat yellow diamond design made especially by Chopard. It is beautiful and, yes, I am very lucky.

I'd chosen to wear a Grecian-style Amanda Wakeley gown that I found in Harvey Nichols. I tried it on and instantly fell in love with it.

Like everyone who throws a party, I was pretty nervous beforehand and panicked because the main party marquee seemed too light and I was afraid no-one was going to dance. In the end, I asked the organizers to turn all the back lights off and felt more relaxed. I'd made a promise to myself that I would have a good time. At my eighteenth I'd spent the majority of the night making sure everyone else was enjoying themselves, but this time I told myself that I'd greet everyone as they came in and then just party the rest of the night away. And that's what I did, for hours and hours, with just a little bit of champagne to fuel me! I partied when the Sugababes came on stage to sing their hits and a special rendition of 'Happy Birthday!' to me; partied when the five-foot, metre-wide, three-tiered birthday cake was wheeled in, decorated with some of my favourite things: a Chloé handbag, Christian Louboutin shoes, Chanel sunglasses, diamonds and a photo of Wayne; and laughed when they couldn't get the cake on stage. I was shouting 'Where's me candle?' until someone picked up a candle from a nearby table and handed it over for me to blow out and make a wish. I stood up on that stage, looking out at everyone I knew, everyone I grew up with, who've known me all my life and … I get goose-bumps just thinking about that night again. It was so lovely. It was a brilliant night. The best night of my life.

Of course, the next day there were stories in the papers. About how the little boxes of fairy cakes I'd given to the girls as a memento were being sold on eBay, for £500 apparently! Then there was Wayne's cousin, Natalie, who flashed her boobs at the paparazzi then told the newspapers Wayne was going to buy her a boob job. And her brother, Stephen, who came out saying he was a drag queen or whatever. It didn't really bother me. If they wanted to make a show of themselves that was up to them. They couldn't spoil what was a fantastic night.

The whole year seemed to have this brilliant momentum all of its own, and both me and Wayne were picked up in the whirlwind thrill of it all. In May Wayne won his first Premiership title medal with Manchester United. For ages he'd been saying to me, 'Imagine if we win the league,' and then they did. He was so made up. On the last day of the season at Old Trafford it was fantastic to see him collecting his medal. Although, I admit, I did feel a bit left out because all the girls with kids went down on the pitch to celebrate. Wayne offered to borrow a baby off his teammate Darren Fletcher because he'd just had twins, but I didn't mind really. I was just dead proud of him.

Speaking of football, last summer was also the year of footballers' weddings. Wayne's club captain, Gary Neville, teammate Michael Carrick, Steven Gerrard and England captain John Terry were all married on the same weekend. In the end, unfortunately, we only managed to make it to two, flying by helicopter down to John Terry's wedding at Blenheim Palace on the Friday, then driving back up north the next day to see Gary Neville and Emma tie the knot at Manchester Cathedral. Both weddings were different, but both were fantastic. John Terry had Lionel Richie playing live in the most gorgeous of settings at Blenheim Palace, and Gary and Emma had a romantic ceremony in Manchester Cathedral and shared part of their day with the Manchester United fans as they entered and left the cathedral. Then we all went back to party the night away in the fantastic grounds of Gary and Emma's home. They were equally lovely days.

The whole year seemed to have this brilliant momentum all of its own, and both me and Wayne were picked up in the whirlwind thrill of it all.

One of the reasons why we weren't able to make it to Michael Carrick's Sunday wedding barbecue was because me and Wayne were flying out to Las Vegas for a holiday. Our friend, the boxer Ricky Hatton, was defending his World Light Welterweight title out there and had asked Wayne to carry his championship belt into the ring beforehand. It was a real honour for him. So the idea was to spend a few days in Las Vegas, then fly on to Hawaii. We'd been on a boat in the south of France earlier in the summer with around ten friends or so, but this was going to be our big summer holiday. In the end, though, we were having such a good time in Las Vegas we decided to spend our whole ten-day holiday there. I could have stayed longer.

We stayed at a new hotel call The Wynn. I was in two minds about Las Vegas. It never really appealed to me as a holiday destination. I just thought it was about the nightlife, 100-degree heat and casinos. Then the two of us flew in there and a load of Wayne's mates – John O'Shea, Wes Brown and Rio – came in later for the big fight, and I thought, 'Ah, Wayne just wants to go out with them!' But it wasn't like that. The hotel was brilliant. It had a private pool surrounded by cabanas that you could hire for the day with TVs in them and everything, and you just met loads of people. You'd go shopping at Caesar's Palace during the day, then you'd go to see a show a night: *Mamma Mia*, Cirque de Soleil, Celine Dion. I'm not really a big Celine Dion fan but Wayne loves all that Celine, Whitney Houston, Mariah Carey kind of music. He likes all different kinds of music, and he loved the way Leona from *The X Factor* sang. I only actually went to play in the casinos once. Wayne wasn't that bothered but I was like, 'C'mon let's have a go on one of these.' I sat down in front of

Watching Celine Dion perform at Caesar's Palace, Las Vegas.

My whole life ahead of me

one of these big fruit machines, put my money in and went to pull the lever. That was the only reason I wanted a go – to pull this lever like a big kid. Then I found out it was fake and you had to press a button! I was well disappointed! And we didn't win.

Ricky did win though. I'd been nervous because Ricky's a big Manchester City fan and Las Vegas was full of his and their supporters. And Manchester City fans don't exactly like Manchester United players. There was talk beforehand of them booing Wayne before the fight. Thankfully, everyone was really friendly and even started shouting 'Rooney' as he made his way to the ring.

It was one of the biggest fights of the year and we were sat ringside with Ricky's family and friends. Wayne was on one side of me shouting his head off and Ricky's girlfriend, Jennifer, on the other. It was all over dead quick but I was so glad he won. Ricky jumped out of the ring, and threw his gumshield towards us. Jennifer caught it and gave it to Wayne. Wayne was made up but I was thinking, 'That's lovely, but it's just come out of his mouth!' They have different ways in boxing, as I discovered. One of the things Ricky likes to do is to spit water at anyone who's new to his gym. That's what happened when Wayne visited him during training and I couldn't get over it. Wayne must have told him, because after the fight Ricky came over with a bottle of water, took a gulp, and spat water all over me. Well, almost. I ducked just in time so most of it missed!

The days afterwards were spent around the pool and going to shows at night. Rio stayed on and it was there that he decided to propose to his girlfriend Rebecca. He was saying to me and

Wayne, 'I'm going to ask Rebecca to marry me,' and I was like, 'Yeah, it would be lovely.' So, Rebecca flew across and Rio asked her to be his wife.

Yes, it's been a busy year and it's going to get busier, but the main thing is I've never been happier.

There was a lot of romance in the air. The day before Rebecca flew over, we met Vinnie Jones and his wife Tanya by the pool – they were there to renew their wedding vows. They were really nice. Me, Wayne and Rio were spending the day at our pool and Vinnie ended up inviting us for a drink to celebrate, and we said, 'Yeah, see you later.' Next thing we know, Vinnie and Tanya had returned from the chapel and were surrounded by all their friends, calling us over to their cabana for a drink. He's wearing the same purple suit he wore the day he first got married and his wife and all the other girls are now dressed up. Everyone's dressed up except us three. I'm in my bikini, Wayne's in his soaking wet flowery swimming shorts and Rio's not looking much smarter in his shorts. We're having a drink and all of a sudden I realize there's an official photographer from *Hello!* there taking pictures of us all. Everyone else was done up really lovely and there was us three not looking so glam. I didn't tell Wayne and Rio until afterwards and they were mortified. It was so funny. Thing is, the pictures came out and we didn't look so bad.

There was a lot of talk about weddings last summer, and that only made me think more and more about my own. It's official, me and Wayne are going to get married this year. We haven't fixed a date yet – that will depend on whether England qualify for the European Championships and by the time you're reading this, I'm really hoping we have – but we are going to get married this summer. In some ways my twenty-first birthday was a bit of a trial run in terms of the organization. I've just started having meetings with the wedding planners but that's as far as things have got. Wayne hasn't been involved much yet. He's so laid back anyway, he'll just say, 'Do whatever you want.' Going to Gary Neville's wedding and John Terry's made me think about our own and you start thinking of little ideas. I really can't wait. No doubt, in the next few months you'll be reading loads of rumours in the press about our marriage plans but, believe me, unless you hear them from either me or Wayne then I'd take them with a pinch of salt. All I will say at this stage is that it's going to be the wedding I've always dreamed of.

It's official, me and Wayne are going to get married this year.

Yes, it's been a busy year and it's going to get busier, but the main thing is I've never been happier. Have I changed? Has all the attention changed me, the new career opportunities and, yeah, the rewards that go with that? Those are the most common questions I'm asked these days. I hope not, is my answer. Maybe Wayne, my mum and dad and my mates are better qualified to answer that question than I am.

I try to be honest with myself. I guess I've had to become more professional in the past twelve months. Not that I didn't try my hardest before, just that now my diary's so full I've had to learn to put a public face on, so to speak. I know I shouldn't moan because life's too short to moan, and I've been given this chance to do a dream job. But, sometimes, I'll return from filming in London, and I've been missing Wayne and Wayne isn't there because he's away playing football, and I'll be plain knackered and moody. My mum and dad see it on the odd occasion. 'What have you been up to?' my mum will ask, and because everything's been going round in my head so much I'll just be thinking, 'I'm too tired. I don't want to talk.' I know you shouldn't be like that, but I can't help myself. I used to be a bit like that, moody and silent, on school mornings and my mum and dad would say, 'Oooh, don't talk to her!' It's wrong, I know, but you can't always control your feelings. So, yes, I admit it, sometimes I can be a bit of a bitch. Not much of one, I hope.

I don't feel any different from how I felt a few years ago. Maybe a little bit wiser in terms of dealing with celebrity and the security issues that come with having a public profile, and sometimes I feel a bit older than my years. But, then again, I am growing up in many ways – after all, I'm going to be married soon. That part of me's growing up. The other side of my life, when I'm with my mates, the same mates I've always had, having a laugh and dancing around, feels the same as when I was sixteen years old. And that's how I like it.

Have I changed? I hope not, because I don't want to change. I just want to be me.

chapter twenty-two

my big list of questions

When I was a kid I always used to love the quick-fire question-naires in magazines, and I still do. Here's a list of a few of my favourite things, my not-so-favourite things, some trivia, with the odd psychological test thrown in for your amusement!

Favourite film?
That's easy. *Grease.*

Favourite actress?
Julia Roberts.

Favourite actor?
Probably Denzel Washington.

Favourite song at the moment?
'Bleeding Love' by Leona Lewis.

Favourite song of all time?

That's a hard one to choose. How about 'Grease mega-hits'.

Favourite book?

Fashion Babylon by Imogen Edwards-Jones and Anonymous.

What makes you laugh?

No question about it, my youngest brother, Anthony. He's great at taking people off, like family and friends, and then he'll just do stupid things that crack me up. He's really funny.

What makes you cry?

I don't cry easily, but, then again, I can watch something like 'The X Factor' and it'll bring tears to my eyes. Especially when the contestants go back to their families to tell them whether they've got through or not.

What makes you depressed?

Being away from friends and family.

What gets you annoyed?

When you're driving in the car and you let someone out and they don't say thank you.

Do you ever have any recurring dreams?

My house getting broken into. They started after Wayne's mum and dad had their house broken into, and ever since then I sometimes have this dream that it's happening to us. It's more of a nightmare than a dream. If I wake up in the middle I have to go to the window to check that no one's there. Mind, in Germany, when I shared a room with Claire at the hotel, she reckoned I used to laugh a lot in my sleep. I don't know what about, but apparently I'd be giggling away to myself!

Let's do an amateur psychological test. You can't think about the answers too much, you've just got to say the first thing that comes into your head.
Okay.

You're in the woods, a thick green forest, when you see an opening. In the opening there's a drinking vessel of some description. What do you see?
A tap. It's an old-fashioned tap, and it's the kind of tap you'd see on a stand-pipe at something like a caravan site.

Okay, you leave the tap behind, re-enter the forest and keep walking until you see another opening. In the opening, there's a bear. What kind of bear do you see?
It's a big brown bear and it's just walking around.

How do you react to it?
I don't know. I don't do anything. I know I'm not scared of it but I'm a bit wary.

You leave the bear behind, return to the forest and continue walking until you see another opening. This time there's water of some kind. What do you see?
A small stream.

What do you do when you see the stream?
I walk past it.

Okay, so you keep walking, back through the forest until you come to a wall. What kind of wall do you see?
A big, high, brick wall.

And what do you do?
I don't know if it's a dead end or not, but I try to climb over.

And do you succeed?
No, it's too high.

That's it. The end.

So what does that mean?

Well, the drinking vessel is meant to represent your view of an ideal partner ...
A tap?!

Something functional and dependable ... The bear is how you see life, the water represents your sex life and the wall is meant to represent your view on the afterlife.

Let's do another one.

Name the first animal that comes into your head.
A giraffe.

And a second?

An elephant.

Finally, a third?

A lion.

The first animal is how you'd like people to see you. The second is how you see yourself. The third is what you really are ...

A lion?!

Favourite colour?

I always used to say green but I don't know why, as it's not. The colour I like most is pink. Pink girly things.

Favourite animal?

A dog.

Any particular kind?

No.

Favourite TV programme?

That would probably be *The X Factor*.

Favourite TV soap?

That's difficult. It's got to be between *EastEnders* and *Coronation Street*. At the moment I'd say *Coronation Street*.

If you could choose an actress to play you in the film of your life who would it be?

Cameron Diaz.

If you could swap places with anyone famous for a day who would you choose?

I think it would have to be the Queen. Just because I'd really love to see what it would be like to be her.

Do you believe in aliens?

No.

Favourite car?

That would have to be the black convertible Bentley Wayne bought me.

Have you ever stolen anything?

No.

Favourite joke?

To be honest, I'm not very good at jokes, and can never remember them. Half the time, I don't even get them. But someone acting stupid gets me laughing straight away.

What's your favourite season of the year?

Summer.

Do you vote Labour, Conservative, Lib Dem or other?

I've never voted. To be honest, I don't know what they all mean.

Favourite flower?

Lily.

Favourite smell?

Well, I like the smell of cut grass, but if we are talking about perfumes I'd have to go for my own (ha ha)!

Have you ever wished you were a man?

No.

If you were invisible for a day what would you do?

I'd be that fly on the wall! Just because I'm nosy!

Have you any special skill or talent that we should know about?

I can do a headstand! Not very special, I know!

What's your worst habit?

That would have to be grinding my teeth during my sleep. Well, that's what Wayne says I do.

Favourite guilty pleasure?

Expensive shoes and bags.

What's your most treasured possession?

My mobile phone.

What's your idea of perfect happiness?

Being healthy and having a family.

Favourite swear word?

I haven't got one. I don't like swear words.

If you could be transported back in time to one era, which one would it be?

I'd love to go back to the early 1970s when all the hippies were around. Just because they all just got on.

Which historical figure do you most admire?

Jesus Christ.

Favourite musician or band?

That's a hard one because I like a bit of everything but my favourite band would have to be The Stereophonics. Wayne got me into them.

Biggest regret?

It must be when I decided to buy a pair of yellow moon boots and I wore them out in public!

Favourite junk food?

McDonald's. The chicken sandwich meal.

Favourite vegetable?

Broccoli.

Most used phrase or word?

I've got to admit I say 'Thingyo' a lot when I can't think of a thingyo. That's a joke! I use it when I can't think of a word.

What's your least favourite smell?

Burps. I hate it when someone burps.

One thing that reminds you of home?

Well, if it's my house then it would be having football constantly on the telly, but at my mum and dad's it would be proper, home-cooked meals.

What's your lucky number?

I just wanted to say seven. I haven't really got a lucky number, but I've always liked the number four for some reason.

What are you scared of?

Rats. I hate them.

What do you regard as your biggest achievement?

That's a difficult one. I'm proud of where I am in my life right now. Otherwise, I would have to say my GCSE results, my book and my perfume.

What's the one thing that always makes you happy?

Being around family.

How would you like to be remembered?

As someone who was happy.

acknowledgements

During my life to date I have received unbelievable love and support from people who mean the world to me and I couldn't finish this book without thanking them.

To Nan and Granddad, who mean so much to me, thank you for your continuous love and support. To all my family, family means everything to me, I love our gatherings and am always looking forward to the next one. To my friends, the Girls, thanks for your friendship, great company and always looking out for me. To Wayne's family, thanks for all your support and friendship throughout the years.

To my agent Paul Stretford, thanks for putting your faith in me, we have come out brilliantly on the other side! You are such a big part of Wayne's and my life. Thank you for everything. To Rach, Steve, Jane, Kona and everyone at Proactive, I would be lost without you! Thanks for keeping everything under control. To my publicists Ian Monk Associates, especially Ian and his team, for your continuous phone calls and emails and putting people straight! Thanks to you all for your hard work – it's something that I appreciate so much.

To Justine and Gerry and everyone at Cricket – what would I do without your great shop, service and friendship? Thanks. Also to everyone who has taught and helped me along the way at my schools, St Teresa's and St John Bosco, especially Miss Tremarco, who always believed in me. Also the Harlequin Dance and Drama School – I had some fantastic times there and made great friends. Thank you to Pat and Craig and everyone involved.

I also couldn't complete this book without a mention of the numerous people I have met and worked with over the past few years – some people I have highlighted, the others know who you are. I thank you all for being a part of making this book possible.

So here goes.

Thanks to all the journalists who have been nice and if not nice then at least fair, to the few PAs who have been understanding instead of pushy – it means a lot. To the photographers, stylists, hair and make-up artists and their assistants, thanks for all your hard work, dedication and professionalism – the results have been worth it. To the directors, cameramen, lighting engineers and numerous assistants and professionals I have worked with, making TV commercials and programmes. Thanks.

To all the brands, magazines and media I have been fortunate enough to work with. I have enjoyed it enormously and hope you did too. I should also make special mention of Jane Johnson, the former editor of *Closer* magazine, who was brave enough to give me my own column. To Karen McGinn and Nathalie McMahon at Asda and George respectively – working with you has been great fun and something that I am very proud of professionally. To everyone at LG phones – love the product and the fantastic pictures. To Steve Cummings and all the Coca Cola GB team – thought the ad looked great in Piccadilly Circus.

To Alexandra Shulman for getting me back out there and helping me re-discover my confidence.

To Sir Trevor McDonald for giving me the opportunity to work on such an important topic and something so close to my heart. On that note, to all the people at both Claire House and Alder Hey Children's Hospital for the work they do caring for sick and needy children and especially the love and care they show my sister. My work with you is something I cherish.

This book would not have been possible without the incredible hard work, professionalism and support of a number of key people.

Harvey, thanks for all your hard work in making this book a reality. You made it such an easy process. I loved working with you again and hope to do so more in the future. To Michael Labica and Sandrine Dulermo for the stunning pictures including the front cover. To all at my publishers HarperCollins, especially Belinda Budge, Sally Potter and Simon Gerratt from the editorial team, Jacqui Caulton and James Annal from the design team, Elizabeth Dawson, Eve Fernandez and Eleanor Goymer, Karen Davies and everybody in the HarperCollins sales team. A really big thank you.

Finally, to everyone who has taken the time to buy and read this book. I hope you enjoyed it and have a better idea of who I really am.

index